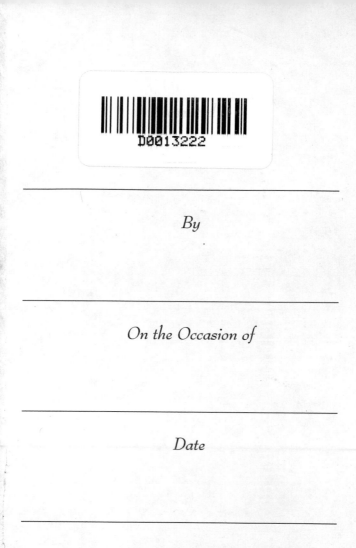

_____

By

_____

On the Occasion of

_____

Date

_____

The
Bible
Promise
Book

King James Version

BARBOUR
PUBLISHING

© MCMXC by Barbour Publishing, Inc.

ISBN 0-916441-43-1

All Scripture quotations are taken from the Authorized King James Version of the Bible.

Published by Barbour Publishing, Inc., P.O. Box 719, Uhrichsville, OH 44683, www.barbourbooks.com

ecpa Member of the
Evangelical Christian
Publishers Association

Printed in the United States of America.

Introduction

Whatever the need of the moment, the answer is to be found in Scripture, if we take the time to search for it. Whatever we're feeling, whatever we're suffering, whatever we're hoping, the Bible has something to say to us.

This collection of Bible verses is meant for use as a handy reference when you need the Bible's guidance on a particular problem in your life. It is in no way intended to replace regular Bible study or the use of a concordance for in-depth study of a subject. There are many facets of your life and many topics in the Bible that are not covered here.

But if you are feeling extremely lonely one day, some of the Bible's wisdom and comfort is available to you here under the topic of *Loneliness*. All topics are arranged alphabetically, for ease of use.

All Scripture is from The King James Version of the Bible.

Contents

Anger

The Lord is gracious, and full of compassion; slow to anger, and of great mercy.   ❧ *Psalm 145:8*

A God ready to pardon, gracious and merciful, slow to anger, and of great kindness. . .

❧ *Nehemiah 9:17*

For his anger endureth but a moment; in his favour is life: weeping may endure for a night, but joy cometh in the morning.   ❧ *Psalm 30:5*

Wherefore, my beloved brethren, let every man be swift to hear, slow to speak, slow to wrath:

For the wrath of man worketh not the righteousness of God.   ❧ *James 1:19–20*

Be not hasty in thy spirit to be angry: for anger resteth in the bosoms of fools.   ❧ *Ecclesiastes 7:9*

He that is soon angry dealeth foolishly.

❧ *Proverbs 14:17*

He that is slow to anger is better than the mighty; and he that ruleth his spirit than he that taketh a city.

❧ *Proverbs 16:32*

A wrathful man stirreth up strife: but he that is slow to anger appeaseth strife.   ❧ *Proverbs 15:18*

An angry man stirreth up strife, and a furious man aboundeth in transgression. ❦ *Proverbs 29:22*

Cease from anger, and forsake wrath: fret not thyself in any wise to do evil. ❦ *Psalm 37:8*

Make no friendship with an angry man; and with a furious man thou shalt not go:
> Lest thou learn his ways, and get a snare to thy soul.
> ❦ *Proverbs 22:24–25*

A soft answer turneth away wrath: but grievous words stir up anger. ❦ *Proverbs 15:1*

Fathers, provoke not your children to anger, lest they be discouraged. ❦ *Colossians 3:21*

Be ye angry, and sin not: let not the sun go down upon your wrath. ❦ *Ephesians 4:26*

The discretion of a man deferreth his anger; and it is his glory to pass over a transgression.
❦ *Proverbs 19:11*

It is better to dwell in the wilderness, than with a contentious and an angry woman. ❦ *Proverbs 21:19*

But I say unto you, That whosoever is angry with his brother without a cause shall be in danger of the judgment. ❦ *Matthew 5:22*

Let all bitterness, and wrath, and anger, and clamour, and evil speaking, be put away from you, with all malice:

And be ye kind one to another, tenderhearted, forgiving one another, even as God for Christ's sake hath forgiven you. ❦ *Ephesians 4:31–32*

Dearly beloved, avenge not yourselves, but rather give place unto wrath: for it is written, Vengeance is mine; I will repay, saith the Lord.

Therefore if thine enemy hunger, feed him; if he thirst, give him drink: for in so doing thou shalt heap coals of fire on his head.

Be not overcome of evil, but overcome evil with good. ❦ *Romans 12:19–21*

If thine enemy be hungry, give him bread to eat; and if he be thirsty, give him water to drink:

For thou shalt heap coals of fire upon his head, and the Lord shall reward thee. ❦ *Proverbs 25:21–22*

Wrath is cruel, and anger is outrageous; but who is able to stand before envy? ❦ *Proverbs 27:4*

But now ye also put off all these; anger, wrath, malice, blasphemy, filthy communication out of your mouth.
❦ *Colossians 3:8*

Belief

For God so loved the world, that he gave his only begotten Son, that whosoever believeth in him should not perish, but have everlasting life. ❦ *John 3:16*

To him give all the prophets witness, that through his name whosoever believeth in him shall receive remission of sins. ❦ *Acts 10:43*

As it is written, Behold, I lay in Sion a stumblingstone and rock of offence: and whosoever believeth on him shall not be ashamed. ❦ *Romans 9:33*

But as many as received him, to them gave he power to become the sons of God, even to them that believe on his name. ❦ *John 1:12*

He that believeth on him is not condemned: but he that believeth not is condemned already, because he hath not believed in the name of the only begotten Son of God. ❦ *John 3:18*

He that believeth on the Son hath everlasting life: and he that believeth not the Son shall not see life; but the wrath of God abideth on him. ❦ *John 3:36*

Wherefore also it is contained in the scripture, Behold, I lay in Sion a chief corner stone, elect, precious: and he that believeth on him shall not be confounded. ❦ *1 Peter 2:6*

And they said, Believe on the Lord Jesus Christ, and thou shalt be saved, and thy house. ❦ *Acts 16:31*

I am come a light into the world, that whosoever believeth on me should not abide in darkness. ❦ *John 12:46*

And Jesus said unto them, I am the bread of life: he that cometh to me shall never hunger; and he that believeth on me shall never thirst. ❦ *John 6:35*

Jesus said unto him, If thou canst believe, all things are possible to him that believeth. ❦ *Mark 9:23*

Jesus saith unto him, Thomas, because thou hast seen me, thou hast believed: blessed are they that have not seen, and yet have believed. ❦ *John 20:29*

Verily, verily, I say unto you, He that believeth on me hath everlasting life. ❦ *John 6:47*

Charity

Blessed is he that considereth the poor: the Lord will deliver him in time of trouble.

The Lord will preserve him, and keep him alive; and he shall be blessed upon the earth: and thou wilt not deliver him unto the will of his enemies.

❦ *Psalm 41:1–2*

He that hath pity upon the poor lendeth unto the Lord; and that which he hath given will he pay him again.

❦ *Proverbs 19:17*

But when thou makest a feast, call the poor, the maimed, the lame, the blind:

And thou shalt be blessed; for they cannot recompense thee: for thou shalt be recompensed at the resurrection of the just. ❦ *Luke 14:13–14*

Sell that ye have, and give alms; provide yourselves bags which wax not old, a treasure in the heavens that faileth not, where no thief approacheth, neither moth corrupteth.

❦ *Luke 12:33*

He that despiseth his neighbour sinneth: but he that hath mercy on the poor, happy is he. ❦ *Proverbs 14:21*

Give, and it shall be given unto you; good measure, pressed down, and shaken together, and running over, shall men give into your bosom. For with the same measure that ye mete withal it shall be measured to you again.

❦ *Luke 6:38*

He hath dispersed, he hath given to the poor; his righteousness endureth for ever; his horn shall be exalted with honour. ❧ *Psalm 112:9*

And now abideth faith, hope, charity, these three; but the greatest of these is charity. ❧ *1 Corinthians 13:13*

He that giveth unto the poor shall not lack: but he that hideth his eyes shall have many a curse.
❧ *Proverbs 28:27*

Every man according as he purposeth in his heart, so let him give; not grudgingly, or of necessity: for God loveth a cheerful giver. ❧ *2 Corinthians 9:7*

There is that scattereth, and yet increaseth; and there is that withholdeth more than is meet, but it tendeth to poverty.
The liberal soul shall be made fat: and he that watereth shall be watered also himself.
❧ *Proverbs 11:24–25*

I have been young, and now am old; yet have I not seen the righteous forsaken, nor his seed begging bread.
❧ *Psalm 37:25*

Charge them that are rich in this world, that they be not highminded, nor trust in uncertain riches, but in the living God, who giveth us richly all things to enjoy;
That they do good, that they be rich in good works, ready to distribute, willing to communicate.
❧ *1 Timothy 6:17–18*

Cast thy bread upon the waters: for thou shalt find it after many days. 🐦 *Ecclesiastes 11:1*

And if thou draw out thy soul to the hungry, and satisfy the afflicted soul; then shall thy light rise in obscurity, and thy darkness be as the noon day.

🐦 *Isaiah 58:10*

It is not to deal thy bread to the hungry, and that thou bring the poor that are cast out to thy house? when thou seest the naked, that thou cover him; and that thou hide not thyself from thine own flesh?

Then shall thy light break forth as the morning, and thine health shall spring forth speedily: and thy righteousness shall go before thee; the glory of the Lord shall be thy rereward. 🐦 *Isaiah 58:7–8*

And the Levite, (because he hath no part nor inheritance with thee,) and the stranger, and the fatherless, and the widow, which are within thy gates, shall come, and shall eat and be satisfied; that the Lord thy God may bless thee in all the work of thine hand which thou doest.

🐦 *Deuteronomy 14:29*

Then Jesus beholding him loved him, and said unto him, One thing thou lackest: go thy way, sell whatsoever thou hast, and give to the poor, and thou shalt have treasure in heaven: and come, take up the cross, and follow me.

🐦 *Mark 10:21*

He is ever merciful, and lendeth; and his seed is blessed.

🐦 *Psalm 37:26*

Take heed that ye do not your alms before men, to be seen of them: otherwise ye have no reward of your Father which is in heaven.

Therefore when thou doest thine alms, do not sound a trumpet before thee, as the hypocrites do in the synagogues and in the streets, that they may have glory of men. Verily I say unto you, They have their reward.

But when thou doest alms, let not thy left hand know what thy right hand doeth:

That thine alms may be in secret: and thy Father which seeth in secret himself shall reward thee openly.

❦ *Matthew 6:1–4*

Then shall the King say unto them on his right hand, Come, ye blessed of my Father, inherit the kingdom prepared for you from the foundation of the world:

For I was an hungred, and ye gave me meat: I was thirsty, and ye gave me drink: I was a stranger, and ye took me in:

Naked, and ye clothed me: I was sick, and ye visited me: I was in prison, and ye came unto me.

Then shall the righteous answer him, saying, Lord, when saw we thee an hungred, and fed thee? or thirsty, and gave thee drink?

When saw we thee a stranger, and took thee in? or naked, and clothed thee?

Or when saw we thee sick, or in prison, and came unto thee?

And the King shall answer and say unto them, Verily I say unto you, Inasmuch as ye have done it unto one of the least of these my brethren, ye have done it unto me.

❦ *Matthew 25:34–40*

Children

And they said, Believe on the Lord Jesus Christ, and thou shalt be saved, and thy house.   ❧ *Acts 16:31*

For the promise is unto you, and to your children, and to all that are afar off, even as many as the Lord our God shall call.   ❧ *Acts 2:39*

And all thy children shall be taught of the Lord; and great shall be the peace of thy children.   ❧ *Isaiah 54:13*

For I will pour water upon him that is thirsty, and floods upon the dry ground: I will pour my spirit upon thy seed, and my blessing upon thy offspring.
    ❧ *Isaiah 44:3*

But when Jesus saw it, he was much displeased, and said unto them, Suffer the little children to come unto to me, and forbid them not: for of such is the kingdom of God.

Verily I say unto you, Whosoever shall not receive the kingdom of God as a little child, he shall not enter therein.

And he took them up in his arms, put his hands upon them, and blessed them.   ❧ *Mark 10:14–16*

Lo, children are an heritage of the Lord: and the fruit of the womb is his reward.

As arrows are in the hand of a mighty man; so are children of the youth.

Happy is the man that hath his quiver full of them: they shall not be ashamed, but they shall speak with the enemies in the gate. 🐦 *Psalm 127:3–5*

Thy wife shall be as a fruitful vine by the sides of thine house: thy children like olive plants round about thy table. 🐦 *Psalm 128:3*

Yet setteth he the poor on high from affliction, and maketh him families like a flock. 🐦 *Psalm 107: 41*

Children's children are the crown of old men; and the glory of children are their fathers. 🐦 *Proverbs 17:6*

Children's Duties

Children, obey your parents in the Lord: for this is right.

Honour thy father and mother; which is the first commandment with promise;

That it may be well with thee, and thou mayest live long on the earth. 🐾 *Ephesians 6:1–3*

Children, obey your parents in all things: for this is well pleasing unto the Lord. 🐾 *Colossians 3:20*

Honour thy father and thy mother.

🐾 *Luke 18:20*

Cursed be he that setteth light by his father or his mother. 🐾 *Deuteronomy 27:16*

Ye shall fear every man his mother, and his father.

🐾 *Leviticus 19:3*

Honour thy father and thy mother, as the Lord thy God hath commanded thee. 🐾 *Deuteronomy 5:16*

My son, keep thy father's commandment, and forsake not the law of thy mother. 🐾 *Proverbs 6:20*

A wise son heareth his father's instruction: but a scorner heareth not rebuke. 🐾 *Proverbs 13:1*

My son, if sinners entice thee, consent thou not.

🐾 *Proverbs 1:10*

A fool despiseth his father's instruction: but he that regardeth reproof is prudent. ❦ *Proverbs 15:5*

Even a child is known by his doings, whether his work be pure, and whether it be right. ❦ *Proverbs 20:11*

A wise son maketh a glad father: but a foolish son is the heaviness of his mother. ❦ *Proverbs 10:1*

Whoso keepeth the law is a wise son: but he that is a companion of riotous men shameth his father.

❦ *Proverbs 28:7*

Now therefore hearken unto me, O ye children: for blessed are they that keep my ways.

Hear instruction, and be wise, and refuse it not.

❦ *Proverbs 8:32–33*

My son, if thine heart be wise, my heart shall rejoice, even mine.

Yea, my reins shall rejoice, when thy lips speak right things. ❦ *Proverbs 23:15–16*

Hearken unto thy father that begat thee, and despise not thy mother when she is old. ❦ *Proverbs 23:22*

The father of the righteous shall greatly rejoice: and he that begetteth a wise child shall have joy of him.

Thy father and thy mother shall be glad, and she that bare thee shall rejoice.

My son, give me thine heart, and let thine eyes observe my ways. ❦ *Proverbs 23:24–26*

Comfort

God is our refuge and strength, a very present help in trouble.

Therefore will not we fear, though the earth be removed, and though the mountains be carried into the midst of the sea;

Though the waters thereof roar and be troubled, though the mountains shake with the swelling thereof.

❦ *Psalm 46:1–3*

Though I walk in the midst of trouble, thou wilt revive me: thou shalt stretch forth thine hand against the wrath of mine enemies, and thy right hand shall save me.

❦ *Psalm 138:7*

The Lord is my rock, and my fortress, and my deliverer; my God, my strength, in whom I will trust; my buckler, and the horn of my salvation, and my high tower.

❦ *Psalm 18:2*

For he hath not despised nor abhorred the affliction of the afflicted; neither hath he hid his face from him; but when he cried unto him, he heard. ❦ *Psalm 22:24*

Though he fall, he shall not be utterly cast down: for the Lord upholdeth him with his hand. ❦ *Psalm 37:24*

The Lord is good, a strong hold in the day of trouble; and he knoweth them that trust in him.

❦ *Nahum 1:7*

But the salvation of the righteous is of the Lord: he is their strength in the time of trouble.   ❦ *Psalm 37:39*

Cast thy burden upon the Lord, and he shall sustain thee: he shall never suffer the righteous to be moved.

   ❦ *Psalm 55:22*

These things I have spoken unto you, that in me ye might have peace. In the world ye shall have tribulation: but be of good cheer; I have overcome the world.

   ❦ *John 16:33*

Come unto me, all ye that labour and are heavy laden, and I will give you rest.   ❦ *Matthew 11:28*

For as the sufferings of Christ abound in us, so our consolation also aboundeth by Christ.

   ❦ *2 Corinthians 1:5*

The Lord also will be a refuge for the oppressed, a refuge in times of trouble.   ❦ *Psalm 9:9*

For the Lord will not cast off for ever:
   But though he cause grief, yet will he have compassion according to the multitude of his mercies.
   For he doth not afflict willingly nor grieve the children of men.   ❦ *Lamentations 3:31–33*

Wait on the Lord: be of good courage, and he shall strengthen thine heart: wait, I say, on the Lord.

   ❦ *Psalm 27:14*

Contentment

A merry heart doeth good like a medicine: but a broken spirit drieth the bones. ❦ *Proverbs 17:22*

Let your conversation be without covetousness; and be content with such things as ye have: for he hath said, I will never leave thee, nor forsake thee.

❦ *Hebrews 13:5*

All the days of the afflicted are evil: but he that is of a merry heart hath a continual feast. ❦ *Proverbs 15:15*

A sound heart is the life of the flesh: but envy the rottenness of the bones. ❦ *Proverbs 14:30*

But godliness with contentment is great gain.

❦ *1 Timothy 6:6*

Let not thine heart envy sinners: but be thou in the fear of the Lord all the day long.

For surely there is an end; and thine expectation shall not be cut off. ❦ *Proverbs 23:17–18*

Correction, God's

For whom the Lord loveth he correcteth; even as a father the son in whom he delighteth.

❦ Proverbs 3:12

Behold, happy is the man whom God correcteth: therefore despise not thou the chastening of the Almighty:

For he maketh sore, and bindeth up: he woundeth, and his hands make whole. *❦ Job 5:17–18*

Blessed is the man whom thou the chastenest, O Lord, and teachest him out of thy law;

Thou that mayest give him rest from the days of adversity, until the pit be digged for the wicked.

❦ Psalm 94:12–13

For which cause we faint not; but though our outward man perish, yet the inward man is renewed day by day.

For our light affliction, which is but for a moment, worketh for us a far more exceeding and eternal weight of glory. *❦ 2 Corinthians 4:16–17*

For they verily for a few days chastened us after their own pleasure; but he for our profit, that we might be partakers of his holiness.

Now no chastening for the present seemeth to be joyous, but grievous: nevertheless afterward it yieldeth the peaceable fruit of righteousness unto them which are exercised thereby. *❦ Hebrews 12:10–11*

For whom the Lord loveth he chasteneth, and scourgeth every son whom he receiveth.

If ye endure chastening, God dealeth with you as with sons; for what son is he whom the father chasteneth not? ❦ *Hebrews 12:6–7*

But when we are judged, we are chastened of the Lord, that we should not be condemned with the world.

❦ *1 Corinthians 11:32*

Courage

Wait on the Lord: be of good courage, and he shall strengthen thine heart: wait, I say, on the Lord.

❧ *Psalm 27:14*

For the Lord loveth judgment, and forsaketh not his saints; they are preserved for ever: but the seed of the wicked shall be cut off. ❧ *Psalm 37:28*

But now thus saith the Lord that created thee, O Jacob, and he that formed thee, O Israel, Fear not: for I have redeemed thee, I have called thee by thy name: thou art mine. ❧ *Isaiah 43:1*

Fear not: for they that be with us are more than they that be with them. ❧ *2 Kings 6:16*

Trust in the Lord, and do good; so shalt thou dwell in the land, and verily thou shalt be fed. ❧ *Psalm 37:3*

He giveth power to the faint; and to them that have no might he increaseth strength. ❧ Isaiah 40:29

Be of good courage, and he shall strengthen your heart, all ye that hope in the Lord. ❧ *Psalm 31:24*

I know both how to be abased, and I know how to abound: every where and in all things I am instructed both to be full and to be hungry, both to abound and to suffer need.

I can do all things through Christ which strengtheneth me. ❧ *Philippians 4:12–13*

Death

Yea, though I walk through the valley of the shadow of death, I will fear no evil: for thou art with me; thy rod and thy staff they comfort me.   ❦ *Psalm 23:4*

O death, where is thy sting? O grave, where is thy victory?   ❦ *1 Corinthians 15:55*

The wicked is driven away in his wickedness: but the righteous hath hope in his death.   ❦ *Proverbs 14:32*

Much more then, being now justified by his blood, we shall be saved from wrath through him.

    ❦ *Romans 5:9*

Forasmuch then as the children are partakers of flesh and blood, he also himself likewise took part of the same; that through death he might destroy him that had the power of death, that is, the devil;

And deliver them who through fear of death were all their lifetime subject to bondage.

    ❦ *Hebrews 2:14–15*

Verily, verily, I say unto you, If a man keep my saying, he shall never see death.   ❦ *John 8:51*

For this God is our God for ever and ever: he will be our guide even unto death.   ❦ *Psalm 48:14*

But God will redeem my soul from the power of the grave: for he shall receive me.   ❦ *Psalm 49:15*

My flesh and my heart faileth: but God is the strength of my heart, and my portion for ever.

❦ Psalm 73:26

He will swallow up death in victory; and the Lord God will wipe away tears from off all faces.   ❦ Isaiah 25:8

I will ransom them from the power of the grave; I will redeem them from death: O death, I will be thy plagues; O grave, I will be thy destruction: repentance shall be hid from mine eyes.   *❦ Hosea 13:14*

Precious in the sight of the LORD is the death of his saints.

❦ Psalm 116:15

Mark the perfect man, and behold the upright: for the end of that man is peace.   *❦ Psalm 37:37*

But though our outward man perish, yet the inward man is renewed day by day.   *❦ 2 Corinthians 4:16*

That whosoever believeth in him should not perish, but have eternal life.   *❦ John 3:15*

For I am persuaded, that neither death, nor life, nor angels, nor principalities, nor powers, nor things present, nor things to come,

Nor height, nor depth, nor any other creature, shall be able to separate us from the love of God, which is in Christ Jesus our Lord.   *❦ Romans 8: 38–39*

Enemies

And the Lord shall help them, and deliver them: he shall deliver them from the wicked, and save them, because they trust in him. 🍎 *Psalm 37:40*

They that hate thee shall be clothed with shame; and the dwelling place of the wicked shall come to nought.
🍎 *Job 8:22*

For the rod of the wicked shall not rest upon the lot of the righteous; lest the righteous put forth their hands unto iniquity. 🍎 *Psalm 125:3*

His heart is established, he shall not be afraid, until he see his desire upon his enemies. 🍎 *Psalm 112:8*

In famine he shall redeem thee from death: and in war from the power of the sword. 🍎 *Job 5:20*

Through God we shall do valiantly: for he it is that shall tread down our enemies. 🍎 *Psalm 60:12*

No weapon that is formed against thee shall prosper; and every tongue that shall rise against thee in judgment thou shalt condemn. This is the heritage of the servants of the Lord, and their righteousness is of me, saith the Lord.
🍎 *Isaiah 54:17*

When a man's ways please the Lord, he maketh even his enemies to be at peace with him. 🍎 *Proverbs 16:7*

The Lord taketh my part with them that help me: therefore shall I see my desire upon them that hate me.

❧ *Psalm 118:7*

That he would grant unto us, that we being delivered out of the hand of our enemies might serve him without fear.

❧ *Luke 1:74*

The Lord shall cause thine enemies that rise up against thee to be smitten before thy face: they shall come out against thee one way, and flee before thee seven ways.

❧ *Deuteronomy 28:7*

For in the time of trouble he shall hide me in his pavilion: in the secret of his tabernacle shall he hide me; he shall set me up upon a rock.

And now shall mine head be lifted up above mine enemies round about me: therefore will I offer in his tabernacle sacrifices of joy; I will sing, yea, I will sing praises unto the Lord.

❧ *Psalm 27: 5–6*

For the Lord your God is he that goeth with you, to fight for you against your enemies, to save you.

❧ *Deuteronomy 20:4*

And shall not God avenge his own elect, which cry day and night unto him, though he bear long with them?

❧ *Luke 18:7*

Behold, they shall surely gather together, but not by me: whosoever shall gather together against thee shall fall for thy sake.

❧ *Isaiah 54:15*

Ye that love the Lord, hate evil: he preserveth the souls of his saints; he delivereth them out of the hand of the wicked.   ❦ *Psalm 97:10*

But I will deliver thee in that day, saith the Lord: and thou shalt not be given into the hand of the men of whom thou art afraid.

    For I will surely deliver thee, and thou shalt not fall by the sword, but thy life shall be for a prey unto thee: because thou hast put thy trust in me, saith the Lord.

      ❦ *Jeremiah 39:17–18*

But the Lord your God ye shall fear; and he shall deliver you out of the hand of all your enemies.

      ❦ *2 Kings 17:39*

And he answered, Fear not: for they that be with us are more than they that be with them.   ❦ *2 Kings 6:16*

Behold, all they that were incensed against thee shall be ashamed and confounded: they shall be as nothing; and they that strive with thee shall perish.

    Thou shalt seek them, and shalt not find them, even them that contended with thee: they that war against thee shall be as nothing, and as a thing of nought.

      ❦ *Isaiah 41:11–12*

Be not afraid of sudden fear, neither of the desolation of the wicked, when it cometh.

    For the Lord shall be thy confidence, and shall keep thy foot from being taken.   ❦ *Proverbs 3:25–26*

That we should be saved from our enemies, and from the hand of all that hate us. 🐞 *Luke 1:71*

For I am with thee, and no man shall set on thee to hurt thee: for I have much people in this city.

🐞 *Acts 18:10*

So that we may boldly say, The Lord is my helper, and I will not fear what man shall do unto me.

🐞 *Hebrews 13:6*

Envy

Neither shalt thou desire thy neighbour's wife, neither shalt thou covet thy neighbour's house, his field, or his manservant, or his maidservant, his ox, or his ass, or any thing that is thy neighbour's.   ❧ *Deuteronomy 5:21*

For where envying and strife is, there is confusion and every evil work.   ❧ *James 3:16*

Do ye think that the scripture saith in vain, The spirit that dwelleth in us lusteth to envy?   ❧ *James 4:5*

Let us not be desirous of vain glory, provoking one another, envying one another.   ❧ *Galatians 5:26*

For the wicked boasteth of his heart's desire, and blesseth the covetous, whom the Lord abhorreth.

❧ *Psalm 10:3*

Envy thou not the oppressor, and choose none of his ways.   ❧ *Proverbs 3:31*

A sound heart is the life of the flesh: but envy the rottenness of the bones.   ❧ *Proverbs 14:30*

Wrath is cruel, and anger is outrageous; but who is able to stand before envy?   ❧ *Proverbs 27:4*

Let no man seek his own, but every man another's wealth.   ❧ *1 Corinthians 10:24*

Rest in the Lord, and wait patiently for him: fret not thyself because of him who prospereth in his way.

❦ *Psalm 37:7*

Again, I considered all travail, and every right work, that for this a man is envied of his neighbour. This is also vanity and vexation of spirit. ❦ *Ecclesiastes 4:4*

Be not thou envious against evil men, neither desire to be with them. ❦ *Proverbs 24:1*

But if ye have bitter envying and strife in your hearts, glory not, and lie not against the truth. ❦ *James 3:14*

Let not thine heart envy sinners: but be thou in the fear of the Lord all the day long.

For surely there is an end; and thine expectation shall not be cut off. ❦ *Proverbs 23:17–18*

And he said unto his disciples, Therefore I say unto you, Take no thought for your life, what ye shall eat; neither for the body, what ye shall put on.

The life is more than meat, and the body is more than raiment. ❦ *Luke 12:22–23*

Eternal Life

Verily, verily I say unto you, He that believeth on me hath everlasting life. 🍎 *John 6:47*

Jesus said unto her, I am the resurrection, and the life: he that believeth in me, though he were dead, yet shall he live:

And whosoever liveth and believeth in me shall never die. Believest thou this? 🍎 *John 11:25–26*

Behold, I shew you a mystery; We shall not all sleep, but we shall all be changed,

In a moment, in the twinkling of an eye, at the last trump: for the trumpet shall sound, and the dead shall be raised incorruptible, and we shall be changed.

For this corruptible must put on incorruption, and this mortal must put on immortality.

So when this corruptible shall have put on incorruption, and this mortal shall have put on immortality, then shall be brought to pass the saying that is written, Death is swallowed up in victory.

🍎 *1 Corinthians 15:51–54*

And this is the promise that he hath promised us, even eternal life. 🍎 *1 John 2:25*

For the Lord himself shall descend from heaven with a shout, with the voice of the archangel, and with the trump of God: and the dead in Christ shall rise first.

🍎 *1 Thessalonians 4:16*

For since by man came death, by man came also the resurrection of the dead. ❦ *1 Corinthians 15:21*

These things have I written unto you that believe on the
name of the Son of God; that ye may know that ye have
eternal life, and that ye may believe on the name of the
Son of God. ❦ *1 John 5:13*

Marvel not at this: for the hour is coming, in the which
all that are in the graves shall hear his voice,

And shall come forth; they that have done good,
unto the resurrection of life; and they that have done
evil, unto the resurrection of damnation.

❦ *John 5:28–29*

Therefore are they before the throne of God, and serve
him day and night in his temple: and he that sitteth on the
throne shall dwell among them.

They shall hunger no more, neither thirst any more;
neither shall the sun light on them, nor any heat.

For the Lamb which is in the midst of the throne
shall feed them, and shall lead them unto living fountains
of waters: and God shall wipe away all tears from their
eyes. ❦ *Revelation 7:15–17*

For God so loved the world, that he gave his only begotten Son, that whosoever believeth in him should not perish, but have everlasting life. ❦ *John 3:16*

For the wages of sin is death; but the gift of God is eternal life through Jesus Christ our Lord.

❦ *Romans 6:23*

So also is the resurrection of the dead. It is sown in corruption; it is raised in incorruption:

It is sown in dishonour; it is raised in glory: it is sown in weakness; it is raised in power:

It is sown a natural body; it is raised a spiritual body. There is a natural body, and there is a spiritual body.

❦ *1 Corinthians 15:42–44*

But if the Spirit of him that raised up Jesus from the dead dwell in you, he that raised up Christ from the dead shall also quicken your mortal bodies by his Spirit that dwelleth in you. ❦ *Romans 8:11*

And God shall wipe away all tears from their eyes; and there shall be no more death, neither sorrow, nor crying, neither shall there be any more pain: for the former things are passed away. ❦ *Revelation 21:4*

And though after my skin worms destroy this body, yet in my flesh shall I see God:

Whom I shall see for myself, and mine eye shall behold, and not another; though my reins be consumed within me. ❦ *Job 19:26–27*

For he that soweth to his flesh shall of the flesh reap corruption; but he that soweth to the Spirit shall of the Spirit reap life everlasting. ❦ *Galatians 6:8*

For we know that if our earthly house of this tabernacle were dissolved, we have a building of God, an house not made with hands, eternal in the heavens.

❦ *2 Corinthians 5:1*

And many of them that sleep in the dust of the earth shall awake, some to everlasting life, and some to shame and everlasting contempt. ❦ *Daniel 12:2*

Thy dead men shall live, together with my dead body shall they arise. Awake and sing, ye that dwell in dust: for thy dew is as the dew of herbs, and the earth shall cast out the dead. ❦ *Isaiah 26:19*

For thou wilt not leave my soul in hell; neither wilt thou suffer thine Holy One to see corruption.

❦ *Psalm 16:10*

But is now made manifest by the appearing of our Saviour Jesus Christ, who hath abolished death, and hath brought life and immortality to light through the gospel. ❦ *2 Timothy 1:10*

And this is the record, that God hath given to us eternal life, and this life is in his Son. ❦ *1 John 5:11*

In my Father's house are many mansions: if it were not so, I would have told you. I go to prepare a place for you.

And if I go and prepare a place for you, I will come again, and receive you unto myself; that where I am, there ye may be also. ❦ *John 14:2–3*

Faith

Now faith is the substance of things hoped for, the evidence of things not seen.   ❦ *Hebrews 11:1*

Watch ye, stand fast in the faith, quit you like men, be strong.   ❦ *1 Corinthians 16:13*

If any of you lack wisdom, let him ask of God, that giveth to all men liberally, and upbraideth not; and it shall be given him.

But let him ask in faith, nothing wavering. For he that wavereth is like a wave of the sea driven with the wind and tossed.   ❦ *James 1:5–6*

As ye have therefore received Christ Jesus the Lord, so walk ye in him:

Rooted and built up in him, and stablished in the faith, as ye have been taught, abounding therein with thanksgiving.   ❦ *Colossians 2:6–7*

For by grace are ye saved through faith; and that not of yourselves: it is the gift of God.   ❦ *Ephesians 2:8*

For ye are all the children of God by faith in Christ Jesus.   ❦ *Galatians 3:26*

The fruit of the Spirit is love, joy, peace, longsuffering, gentleness, goodness, faith,

Meekness, temperance: against such there is no law.   ❦ *Galatians 5:22–23*

But continue thou in the things which thou hast learned and hast been assured of, knowing of whom thou hast learned them;

And that from a child thou hast known the holy scriptures, which are able to make thee wise unto salvation through faith which is in Christ Jesus.

❦ 2 Timothy 3:14–15

For we walk by faith, not by sight.

❦ 2 Corinthians 5:7

And Jesus answering saith unto them, Have faith in God.

For verily I say unto you, That whosoever shall say unto this mountain, Be thou removed, and be thou cast into the sea; and shall not doubt in his heart, but shall believe that those things which he saith shall come to pass; he shall have whatsoever he saith.

❦ Mark 11:22–23

That Christ may dwell in your hearts by faith; that ye, being rooted and grounded in love,

May be able to comprehend with all saints what is the breadth, and length, and depth, and height;

And to know the love of Christ, which passeth knowledge, that ye might be filled with all the fulness of God.

❦ Ephesians 3:17–19

I am crucified with Christ: nevertheless I live; yet not I, but Christ liveth in me: and the life which I now live in the flesh I live by the faith of the Son of God, who loved me, and gave himself for me.

❦ Galatians 2:20

He that cometh to God must believe that he is, and that he is a rewarder of them that diligently seek him.

❦ *Hebrews 11:6*

Wherefore seeing we also are compassed about with so great a cloud of witnesses, let us lay aside every weight, and the sin which doth so easily beset us, and let us run with patience the race that is set before us,

Looking unto Jesus the author and finisher of our faith; who for the joy that was set before him endured the cross, despising the shame, and is set down at the right hand of the throne of God. ❦ *Hebrews 12:1–2*

Faithfulness, God's

Know therefore that the Lord thy God, he is God, the faithful God, which keepeth covenant and mercy with them that love him and keep his commandments to a thousand generations. 🐦 *Deuteronomy 7:9*

(For the Lord thy God is a merciful God;) he will not forsake thee, neither destroy thee, nor forget the covenant of thy fathers which he sware unto them.
🐦 *Deuteronomy 4:31*

He hath remembered his covenant for ever, the word which he commanded to a thousand generations.
🐦 *Psalm 105:8*

God is not a man, that he should lie; neither the son of man, that he should repent: hath he said, and shall he not do it? or hath he spoken, and shall he not make it good?
🐦 *Numbers 23:19*

Let us hold fast the profession of our faith without wavering; (for he is faithful that promised;).
🐦 *Hebrews 10:23*

If we believe not, yet he abideth faithful: he cannot deny himself. 🐦 *2 Timothy 2:13*

The Lord is not slack concerning his promise, as some men count slackness; but is longsuffering to us-ward.
🐦 *2 Peter 3:9*

Blessed be the Lord, that hath given rest unto his people Israel, according to all that he promised: there hath not failed one word of all his good promise.

❦ 1 Kings 8:56

O Lord, thou art my God; I will exalt thee, I will praise thy name; for thou hast done wonderful things; thy counsels of old are faithfulness and truth. *❦ Isaiah 25:1*

And they that know thy name will put their trust in thee: for thou, Lord, hast not forsaken them that seek thee.

❦ Psalm 9:10

Thy word is true from the beginning: and every one of thy righteous judgments endureth for ever.

❦ Psalm 119:160

For ever, O Lord, thy word is settled in heaven.
Thy faithfulness is unto all generations.

❦ Psalm 119:89–90

And also the Strength of Israel will not lie nor repent: for he is not a man, that he should repent.

❦ 1 Samuel 15:29

For all the promises of God in him are yea, and in him Amen, unto the glory of God by us.

❦ 2 Corinthians 1:20

My covenant will I not break, nor alter the thing that is gone out of my lips. *❦ Psalm 89:34*

Fear

And he said unto them, Why are ye so fearful? how is it that ye have no faith? ❦ *Mark 4:40*

Fear not, little flock; for it is your Father's good pleasure to give you the kingdom. ❦ *Luke 12:32*

For I the Lord thy God will hold thy right hand, saying unto thee, Fear not; I will help thee. ❦ *Isaiah 41:13*

But whoso hearkeneth unto me shall dwell safely, and shall be quiet from fear of evil. ❦ *Proverbs 1:33*

And fear not them which kill the body, but are not able to kill the soul. ❦ *Matthew 10:28*

Be not afraid of sudden fear, neither of the desolation of the wicked, when it cometh.

For the Lord shall be thy confidence, and shall keep thy foot from being taken. ❦ *Proverbs 3:25–26*

For God hath not given us the spirit of fear; but of power, and of love, and of a sound mind.

❦ *2 Timothy 1:7*

The Lord shall give thee rest from thy sorrow, and from thy fear, and from the hard bondage wherein thou wast made to serve. ❦ *Isaiah 14:3*

When thou liest down, thou shalt not be afraid: yea, thou shalt lie down, and thy sleep shall be sweet.

❦ *Proverbs 3:24*

For the eyes of the Lord are over the righteous, and his ears are open unto their prayers: but the face of the Lord is against them that do evil.

And who is he that will harm you, if ye be followers of that which is good?

But and if ye suffer for righteousness' sake, happy are ye: and be not afraid of their terror, neither be troubled.

❦ *1 Peter 3:12–14*

In righteousness shalt thou be established: thou shalt be far from oppression; for thou shalt not fear: and from terror; for it shall not come near thee.

❦ *Isaiah 54:14*

For ye have not received the spirit of bondage again to fear; but ye have received the Spirit of adoption, whereby we cry, Abba, Father.

❦ *Romans 8:15*

So that we may boldly say, The Lord is my helper, and I will not fear what man shall do unto me.

❦ *Hebrews 13:6*

God is our refuge and strength, a very present help in trouble.

❦ *Psalm 46:1*

The fear of man bringeth a snare: but whoso putteth his trust in the Lord shall be safe.

❦ *Proverbs 29:25*

I, even I, am he that comforteth you: who art thou, that thou shouldest be afraid of a man that shall die, and of the son of man which shall be made as grass.

❦ *Isaiah 51:12*

He shall cover thee with his feathers, and under his wings shalt thou trust: his truth shall be thy shield and buckler.

Thou shalt not be afraid for the terror by night; nor for the arrow that flieth by day;

Nor for the pestilence that walketh in darkness; nor for the destruction that wasteth at noonday.

❦ *Psalm 91:4–6*

Fear not; for thou shalt not be ashamed: neither be thou confounded. ❦ *Isaiah 54:4*

When thou passest through the waters, I will be with thee; and through the rivers, they shall not overflow thee: when thou walkest through the fire, thou shalt not be burned; neither shall the flame kindle upon thee. ❦ *Isaiah 43:2*

Peace I leave with you, my peace I give unto you: not as the world giveth, give I unto you. Let not your heart be troubled, neither let it be afraid. ❦ *John 14:27*

Yea, though I walk through the valley of the shadow of death, I will fear no evil: for thou art with me; thy rod and thy staff they comfort me.

Thou preparest a table before me in the presence of mine enemies: thou anointest my head with oil; my cup runneth over. ❦ *Psalm 23: 4–5*

Food and Clothing

And ye shall eat in plenty, and be satisfied, and praise the name of the Lord your God, that hath dealt wondrously with you: and my people shall never be ashamed.

❦ *Joel 2:26*

He maketh peace in thy borders, and filleth thee with the finest of the wheat. ❦ *Psalm 147:14*

He hath given meat unto them that fear him: he will ever be mindful of his covenant. ❦ *Psalm 111:5*

The righteous eateth to the satisfying of his soul: but the belly of the wicked shall want. ❦ *Proverbs 13:25*

I will abundantly bless her provision: I will satisfy her poor with bread. ❦ *Psalm 132:15*

Therefore take no thought, saying, What shall we eat? or, What shall we drink? or, Wherewithal shall we be clothed?

(For after all these things do the Gentiles seek:) for your heavenly Father knoweth that ye have need of all these things. ❦ *Matthew 6:31–32*

Forgiveness

But I say unto you, Love your enemies, bless them that curse you, do good to them that hate you, and pray for them which despitefully use you, and persecute you;

That ye may be the children of your Father which is in heaven: for he maketh his sun to rise on the evil and on the good, and sendeth rain on the just and on the unjust.

❦ *Matthew 5:44–45*

And when ye stand praying, forgive, if ye have ought against any: that your Father also which is in heaven may forgive you your trespasses.

But if ye do not forgive, neither will your Father which is in heaven forgive your trespasses.

❦ *Mark 11:25–26*

For if ye forgive men their trespasses, your heavenly Father will also forgive you. ❦ *Matthew 6:14*

Therefore if thine enemy hunger, feed him; if he thirst, give him drink. ❦ *Romans 12:20*

But love ye your enemies, and do good, and lend, hoping for nothing again; and your reward shall be great, and ye shall be the children of the Highest: for he is kind unto the unthankful and to the evil.

Be ye therefore merciful, as your Father also is merciful.

Judge not, and ye shall not be judged: condemn not, and ye shall not be condemned: forgive, and ye shall be forgiven. ❦ *Luke 6:35–38*

Fruitfulness

I am the true vine, and my father is the husbandman.

Every branch in me that beareth not fruit he taketh away: and every branch that beareth fruit, he purgeth it, that it may bring forth more fruit.

Now ye are clean through the word which I have spoken unto you.

Abide in me, and I in you. As the branch cannot bear fruit of itself, except it abide in the vine; no more can ye, except ye abide in me.

I am the vine, ye are the branches: He that abideth in me, and I in him, the same bringeth forth much fruit: for without me ye can do nothing. ❦ *John 15:1–5*

And he shall be like a tree planted by the rivers of water, that bringeth forth his fruit in his season; his leaf also shall not wither; and whatsoever he doeth shall prosper.

❦ *Psalm 1:3*

Therefore they shall come and sing in the height of Zion, and shall flow together to the goodness of the Lord, for wheat, and for wine, and for oil, and for the young of the flock and of the herd: and their soul shall be as a watered garden; and they shall not sorrow any more at all.

❦ *Jeremiah 31:12*

They shall still bring forth fruit in old age; they shall be fat and flourishing. ❦ *Psalm 92:14*

I will be as the dew unto Israel: he shall grow as the lily, and cast forth his roots as Lebanon.   ❦ *Hosea 14:5*

For if these things be in you, and abound, they make you that ye shall neither be barren nor unfruitful in the knowledge of our Lord Jesus Christ.   ❦ *2 Peter 1:8*

Gossip

Thou shalt not go up and down as a talebearer among thy people: neither shalt thou stand against the blood of thy neighbour: I am the Lord. ❦ *Leviticus 19:16*

The words of a talebearer are as wounds, and they go down into the innermost parts of the belly.

❦ *Proverbs 18:8*

He that goeth about as a talebearer revealeth secrets: therefore meddle not with him that flattereth with his lips. ❦ *Proverbs 20:19*

A talebearer revealeth secrets: but he that is of a faithful spirit concealeth the matter. ❦ *Proverbs 11:13*

A froward man soweth strife: and a whisperer separateth chief friends. ❦ *Proverbs 16:28*

Thy tongue deviseth mischiefs; like a sharp razor, working deceitfully. ❦ *Psalm 52:2*

Where no wood is, there the fire goeth out: so where there is no talebearer, the strife ceaseth.

As coals are to burning coals, and wood to fire; so is a contentious man to kindle strife.

The words of a talebearer are as wounds, and they go down into the innermost parts of the belly.

❦ *Proverbs 26:20–22*

The north wind driveth away rain: so doth an angry countenance a backbiting tongue. 🍂 *Proverbs 25:23*

Keep thy tongue from evil, and thy lips from speaking guile. 🍂 *Psalm 34:13*

Grace, Growth in

Herein is my Father glorified, that ye bear much fruit; so shall ye be my disciples.   ❦ *John 15:8*

And this I pray, that your love may abound yet more and more in knowledge and in all judgment.

    ❦ *Philippians 1:9*

Being filled with the fruits of righteousness, which are by Jesus Christ, unto the glory and praise of God.

    ❦ *Philippians 1:11*

But we all, with open face beholding as in a glass the glory of the Lord, are changed into the same image from glory to glory, even as by the Spirit of the Lord.

    ❦ *2 Corinthians 3:18*

The Lord will perfect that which concerneth me: thy mercy, O Lord, endureth for ever: forsake not the works of thine own hands.   ❦ *Psalm 138:8*

But the path of the just is as the shining light, that shineth more and more unto the perfect day.

    ❦ *Proverbs 4:18*

Which is come unto you, as it is in all the world; and bringeth forth fruit, as it doth also in you, since the day ye heard of it, and knew the grace of God in truth.

    ❦ *Colossians 1:6*

I press toward the mark for the prize of the high calling of God in Christ Jesus.

Let us therefore, as many as be perfect, be thus minded: and if in any thing ye be otherwise minded, God shall reveal even this unto you.

Nevertheless, whereto we have already attained, let us walk by the same rule, let us mind the same thing.

❦ *Philippians 3:14–16*

Furthermore then we beseech you, brethren, and exhort you by the Lord Jesus, that as ye have received of us how ye ought to walk and to please God, so ye would abound more and more. ❦ *1 Thessalonians 4:1*

We are bound to thank God always for you, brethren, as it is meet, because that your faith groweth exceedingly, and the charity of every one of you all toward each other aboundeth. ❦ *2 Thessalonians 1:3*

And beside this, giving all diligence, add to your faith virtue; and to virtue knowledge. ❦ *2 Peter 1:5*

The righteous also shall hold on his way, and he that hath clean hands shall be stronger and stronger.

❦ *Job 17:9*

Guidance

And thine ears shall hear a word behind thee, saying, This is the way, walk ye in it, when ye turn to the right hand, and when ye turn to the left. ❦ *Isaiah 30:21*

For this God is our God for ever and ever: he will be our guide even unto death. ❦ *Psalm 48:14*

A man's heart deviseth his way: but the Lord directeth his steps. ❦ *Proverbs 16:9*

The steps of a good man are ordered by the Lord: and he delighteth in his way. ❦ *Psalm 37:23*

For his God doth instruct him to discretion, and doth teach him. ❦ *Isaiah 28:26*

The righteousness of the perfect shall direct his way: but the wicked shall fall by his own wickedness.
❦ *Proverbs 11:5*

In all thy ways acknowledge him, and he shall direct thy paths. ❦ *Proverbs 3:6*

And I will bring the blind by a way that they knew not; I will lead them in the paths that they have not known: I will make darkness light before them, and crooked things straight. These things will I do unto them, and not forsake them. ❦ *Isaiah 42:16*

Guilt

If we confess our sins, he is faithful and just to forgive us our sins, and to cleanse us from all unrighteousness.

❧ *1 John 1:9*

Let the wicked forsake his way, and the unrighteous man his thoughts: and let him return unto the Lord, and he will have mercy upon him; and to our God, for he will abundantly pardon. ❧ *Isaiah 55:7*

For the Lord your God is gracious and merciful, and will not turn away his face from you, if ye return unto him.

❧ *2 Chronicles 30:9*

As far as the east is from the west, so far hath he removed our transgressions from us. ❧ *Psalm 103:12*

For if our heart condemn us, God is greater than our heart, and knoweth all things. ❧ *1 John 3:20*

For I will be merciful to their unrighteousness, and their sins and their iniquities will I remember no more.

❧ *Hebrews 8:12*

Therefore if any man be in Christ, he is a new creature: old things are passed away; behold, all things are become new. ❧ *2 Corinthians 5:17*

For I will forgive their iniquity, and I will remember their sin no more. ❧ *Jeremiah 31:34*

And I will cleanse them from all their iniquity, whereby they have sinned against me; and I will pardon all their iniquities, whereby they have sinned, and whereby they have transgressed against me. ❦ *Jeremiah 33:8*

I write unto you, little children, because your sins are forgiven you for his name's sake. ❦ *1 John 2:12*

I, even I, am he that blotteth out thy transgressions for mine own sake, and will not remember thy sins.
❦ *Isaiah 43:25*

But if we walk in the light, as he is in the light, we have fellowship one with another, and the blood of Jesus Christ his Son cleanseth us from all sin.
❦ *1 John 1:7*

Help in Troubles

But the salvation of the righteous is of the Lord: he is their strength in the time of trouble.   ❦ *Psalm 37:39*

The Lord openeth the eyes of the blind: the Lord raiseth them that are bowed down: the Lord loveth the righteous.
   ❦ *Psalm 146:8*

The Lord is good, a strong hold in the day of trouble; and he knoweth them that trust in him.   ❦ *Nahum 1:7*

Though he fall, he shall not be utterly cast down: for the Lord upholdeth him with his hand.   ❦ *Psalm 37:24*

Thou art my hiding place; thou shalt preserve me from trouble; thou shalt compass me about with songs of deliverance.   ❦ *Psalm 32:7*

Thou, which hast shewed me great and sore troubles, shalt quicken me again, and shalt bring me up again from the depths of the earth.   ❦ *Psalm 71:20*

Why art thou cast down, O my soul? and why art thou disquieted within me? hope thou in God: for I shall yet praise him, who is the health of my countenance, and my God.   ❦ *Psalm 42:11*

My flesh and my heart faileth: but God is the strength of my heart, and my portion for ever.   ❦ *Psalm 73:26*

There shall no evil befall thee, neither shall any plague come nigh thy dwelling.

For he shall give his angels charge over thee, to keep thee in all thy ways.   ❧ *Psalm 91:10–11*

They that sow in tears shall reap in joy.

He that goeth forth and weepeth, bearing precious seed, shall doubtless come again with rejoicing, bringing his sheaves with him.   ❧ *Psalm 126:5–6*

O love the Lord, all ye his saints: for the Lord preserveth the faithful, and plentifully rewardeth the proud doer.
    ❧ *Psalm 31:23*

Though ye have lien among the pots, yet shall ye be as the wings of a dove covered with silver, and her feathers with yellow gold.   ❧ *Psalm 68:13*

Behold, God will not cast away a perfect man, neither will he help the evildoers:

Till he fill thy mouth with laughing, and thy lips with rejoicing.   ❧ *Job 8:20–21*

He shall deliver thee in six troubles: yea, in seven there shall no evil touch thee.   ❧ *Job 5:19*

For he hath not despised nor abhorred the affliction of the afflicted; neither hath he hid his face from him; but when he cried unto him, he heard.   ❧ *Psalm 22:24*

The Lord also will be a refuge for the oppressed, a refuge in times of trouble.   ❧ *Psalm 9:9*

Though I walk in the midst of trouble, thou wilt revive me: thou shalt stretch forth thine hand against the wrath of mine enemies, and thy right hand shall save me.

❦ Psalm 138:7

Many are the afflictions of the righteous: but the Lord delivereth him out of them all. *❦ Psalm 34:19*

For the Lord will not cast off for ever:

But though he cause grief, yet will he have compassion according to the multitude of his mercies.

For he doth not afflict willingly nor grieve the children of men. *❦ Lamentations 3:31–33*

The Lord is my rock, and my fortress, and my deliverer; my God, my strength, in whom I will trust; my buckler, and the horn of my salvation, and my high tower.

❦ Psalm 18:2

Rejoice not against me, O mine enemy: when I fall, I shall arise; when I sit in darkness, the Lord shall be a light unto me.

I will bear the indignation of the Lord, because I have sinned against him, until he plead my cause, and execute judgment for me: he will bring me forth to the light, and I shall behold his righteousness.

❦ Micah 7:8–9

These things I have spoken unto you, that in me ye might have peace. In the world ye shall have tribulation: but be of good cheer; I have overcome the world.

❦ John 16:33

Holy Spirit

Behold, I will pour out my spirit unto you, I will make known my words unto you. 🥀 *Proverbs 1:23*

And I will pray the Father, and he shall give you another Comforter, that he may abide with you for ever;

Even the Spirit of truth; whom the world cannot receive, because it seeth him not, neither knoweth him: but ye know him; for he dwelleth with you, and shall be in you. 🥀 *John 14:16–17*

He that believeth on me, as the scripture hath said, out of his belly shall flow rivers of living water.

(But this spake he of the Spirit, which they that believe on him should receive: for the Holy Ghost was not yet given; because that Jesus was not yet glorified.) 🥀 *John 7:38–39*

Howbeit when he, the Spirit of truth, is come, he will guide you into all truth: for he shall not speak of himself; but whatsoever he shall hear, that shall he speak: and he will shew you things to come. 🥀 *John 16:13*

As for me, this is my convenant with them, saith the Lord; My spirit that is upon thee, and my words which I have put in thy mouth, shall not depart out of thy mouth, nor out of the mouth of thy seed, nor out of the mouth of thy seed's seed, saith the Lord, from henceforth and for ever. 🥀 *Isaiah 59:21*

If ye then, being evil, know how to give good gifts unto your children: how much more shall your heavenly Father give the Holy Spirit to them that ask him?

❦ *Luke 11:13*

But whosoever drinketh of the water that I shall give him shall never thirst; but the water that I shall give him shall be in him a well of water springing up into everlasting life. ❦ *John 4:14*

And I will put my spirit within you, and cause you to walk in my statutes, and ye shall keep my judgments, and do them. ❦ *Ezekiel 36:27*

That the blessing of Abraham might come on the Gentiles through Jesus Christ; that we might receive the promise of the Spirit through faith. ❦ *Galatians 3:14*

But the anointing which ye have received of him abideth in you, and ye need not that any man teach you: but as the same anointing teacheth you of all things, and is truth, and is no lie, and even as it hath taught you, ye shall abide in him. ❦ *1 John 2:27*

Likewise the Spirit also helpeth our infirmities: for we know not what we should pray for as we ought: but the Spirit itself maketh intercession for us with groanings which cannot be uttered.

And he that searcheth the hearts knoweth what is the mind of the Spirit, because he maketh intercession for the saints according to the will of God.

❦ *Romans 8:26–27*

For the kingdom of God is not meat and drink; but righteousness, and peace, and joy in the Holy Ghost.

❦ *Romans 14:17*

For ye have not received the spirit of bondage again to fear; but ye have received the Spirit of adoption, whereby we cry, Abba, Father.

❦ *Romans 8:15*

Honesty

Ye shall not steal, neither deal falsely, neither lie one to another. *❧ Leviticus 19:11*

Are there yet the treasures of wickedness in the house of the wicked, and the scant measure that is abominable?

Shall I count them pure with the wicked balances, and with the bag of deceitful weights?

For the rich men thereof are full of violence, and the inhabitants thereof have spoken lies, and their tongue is deceitful in their mouth. *❧ Micah 6:10–12*

Ye shall do no unrighteousness in judgment, in meteyard, in weight, or in measure. *❧ Leviticus 19:35*

A false balance is abomination to the Lord: but a just weight is his delight. *❧ Proverbs 11:1*

But thou shalt have a perfect and just weight, a perfect and just measure shalt thou have: that thy days may be lengthened in the land which the Lord thy God giveth thee.

For all that do such things, and all that do unrighteously, are an abomination unto the Lord thy God. *❧ Deuteronomy 25:15–16*

That no man go beyond and defraud his brother in any matter: because that the Lord is the avenger of all such, as we also have forewarned you and testified.

For God hath not called us unto uncleanness, but unto holiness. *❧ 1 Thessalonians 4:6–7*

Lie not one to another, seeing that ye have put off the old man with his deeds;

And have put on the new man, which is renewed in knowledge after the image of him that created him.

❦ *Colossians 3:9–10*

The wicked borroweth, and payeth not again: but the righteous sheweth mercy, and giveth. ❦ *Psalm 37:21*

Withhold not good from them to whom it is due, when it is in the power of thine hand to do it.

❦ *Proverbs 3:27*

And if thou sell aught unto thy neighbour, or buyest aught of thy neighbour's hand, ye shall not oppress one another. ❦ *Leviticus 25:14*

Ye shall not therefore oppress one another; but thou shalt fear thy God: for I am the Lord your God.

❦ *Leviticus 25:17*

Better is a little with righteousness than great revenues without right. ❦ *Proverbs 16:8*

He that walketh righteously, and speaketh uprightly; he that despiseth the gain of oppressions, that shaketh his hands from holding of bribes, that stoppeth his ears from hearing of blood, and shutteth his eyes from seeing evil;

He shall dwell on high: his place of defence shall be the munitions of rocks: bread shall be given him; his waters shall be sure. ❦ *Isaiah 33:15–16*

Hope

Why art thou cast down, O my soul? and why art thou disquieted within me? hope thou in God: for I shall yet praise him, who is the health of my countenance, and my God. ❧ *Psalm 42:11*

Who by him do believe in God, that raised him up from the dead, and gave him glory; that your faith and hope might be in God. ❧ *1 Peter 1:21*

Wherefore gird up the loins of your mind, be sober, and hope to the end for the grace that is to be brought unto you at the revelation of Jesus Christ.
❧ *1 Peter 1:13*

And every man that hath this hope in him purifieth himself, even as he is pure. ❧ *1 John 3:3*

The wicked is driven away in his wickedness: but the righteous hath hope in his death. ❧ *Proverbs 14:32*

For the hope which is laid up for you in heaven, whereof ye heard before in the word of the truth of the gospel. . .
❧ *Colossians 1:5*

Which is Christ in you, the hope of glory.
❧ *Colossians 1:27*

Be of good courage, and he shall strengthen your heart, all ye that hope in the Lord. ❧ *Psalm 31:24*

For thou art my hope, O Lord God: thou art my trust from my youth.   ❧ *Psalm 71:5*

Blessed be the God and Father of our Lord Jesus Christ, which according to his abundant mercy hath begotten us again unto a lively hope by the resurrection of Jesus Christ from the dead.   ❧ *1 Peter 1:3*

Hospitality

Use hospitality one to another without grudging.

As every man hath received the gift, even so minister the same one to another, as good stewards of the manifold grace of God.   ❦ *1 Peter 4:9–10*

If a brother or sister be naked, and destitute of daily food,

And one of you say unto them, Depart in peace, be ye warmed and filled; notwithstanding ye give them not those things which are needful to the body; what doth it profit?   ❦ *James 2:15–16*

For whosoever shall give you a cup of water to drink in my name, because ye belong to Christ, verily I say unto you, he shall not lose his reward.   ❦ *Mark 9:41*

I have shewed you all things, how that so labouring ye ought to support the weak, and to remember the words of the Lord Jesus, how he said, It is more blessed to give than to receive.   ❦ *Acts 20:35*

But whoso hath this world's good, and seeth his brother have need, and shutteth up his bowels of compassion from him, how dwelleth the love of God in him?   ❦ *1 John 3:17*

And the King shall answer and say unto them, Verily I say unto you, Inasmuch as ye have done it unto one of the least of these my brethren, ye have done it unto me.   ❦ *Matthew 25:40*

Be not forgetful to entertain strangers: for thereby some have entertained angels unawares.   ❦ *Hebrews 13:2*

For I mean not that other men be eased, and ye burdened:
     But by an equality, that now at this time your abundance may be a supply for their want, that their abundance also may be a supply for your want: that there may be equality.   ❦ *2 Corinthians 8:13–14*

Distributing to the necessity of saints; given to hospitality.
     ❦ *Romans 12:13*

For I was an hungred, and ye gave me meat: I was thirsty, and ye gave me drink: I was a stranger, and ye took me in:
     Naked, and ye clothed me: I was sick, and ye visited me: I was in prison, and ye came unto me.
     ❦ *Matthew 25:35–36*

Humility

Whosoever therefore shall humble himself as this little child, the same is greatest in the kingdom of heaven.

❧ *Matthew 18:4*

Lord, thou hast heard the desire of the humble: thou wilt prepare their heart, thou wilt cause thine ear to hear.

❧ *Psalm 10:17*

And whosoever shall exalt himself shall be abased; and he that shall humble himself shall be exalted.

❧ *Matthew 23:12*

When men are cast down, then thou shalt say, There is lifting up; and he shall save the humble person.

❧ *Job 22:29*

Better it is to be of an humble spirit with the lowly, than to divide the spoil with the proud.

❧ *Proverbs 16:19*

But he giveth more grace. Wherefore he saith, God resisteth the proud, but giveth grace unto the humble.

❧ *James 4:6*

When he maketh inquisition for blood, he remembereth them: he forgetteth not the cry of the humble.

❧ *Psalm 9:12*

By humility and the fear of the Lord are riches, and honour, and life. ❦ *Proverbs 22:4*

Surely he scorneth the scorners: but he giveth grace unto the lowly. ❦ *Proverbs 3:34*

The fear of the Lord is the instruction of wisdom; and before honour is humility. ❦ *Proverbs 15:33*

A man's pride shall bring him low: but honour shall uphold the humble in spirit. ❦ *Proverbs 29:23*

Humble yourselves therefore under the mighty hand of God, that he may exalt you in due time.

❦ *1 Peter 5:6*

Joy

For ye shall go out with joy, and be led forth with peace:
the mountains and the hills shall break forth before you
into singing, and all the trees of the field shall clap their
hands. ❧ *Isaiah 55:12*

Blessed is the people that know the joyful sound: they
shall walk, O Lord, in the light of thy countenance.
    In thy name shall they rejoice all the day: in thy righ-
teousness shall they be exalted. ❧ *Psalm 89:15–16*

The voice of rejoicing and salvation is in the tabernacles
of the righteous: the right hand of the Lord doeth valiantly.
❧ *Psalm 118:15*

Thou hast put gladness in my heart, more than in the time
that their corn and their wine increased. ❧ *Psalm 4:7*

They that sow in tears shall reap in joy.
    He that goeth forth and weepeth, bearing precious
seed, shall doubtless come again with rejoicing, bringing
his sheaves with him. ❧ *Psalm 126:5–6*

These things have I spoken unto you, that my joy might
remain in you, and that your joy might be full.
❧ *John 15:11*

For then shalt thou have thy delight in the Almighty, and
shalt lift up thy face unto God. ❧ *Job 22:26*

Light is sown for the righteous, and gladness for the upright in heart.

Rejoice in the Lord, ye righteous; and give thanks at the remembrance of his holiness.   ❦ *Psalm 97: 11–12*

Yet I will rejoice in the Lord, I will joy in the God of my salvation.   ❦ *Habakkuk 3:18*

Therefore the redeemed of the Lord shall return, and come with singing unto Zion; and everlasting joy shall be upon their head: they shall obtain gladness and joy; and sorrow and mourning shall flee away.   ❦ *Isaiah 51:11*

For our heart shall rejoice in him, because we have trusted in his holy name.   ❦ *Psalm 33:21*

Whom having not seen, ye love; in whom, though now ye see him not, yet believing, ye rejoice with joy unspeakable and full of glory.   ❦ *1 Peter 1:8*

I will greatly rejoice in the Lord, my soul shall be joyful in my God; for he hath clothed me with the garments of salvation, he hath covered me with the robe of righteousness, as a bridegroom decketh himself with ornaments, and as a bride adorneth herself with her jewels.

❦ *Isaiah 61:10*

Then he said unto them, Go your way, eat the fat, and drink the sweet, and send portions unto them for whom nothing is prepared: for this day is holy unto our Lord: neither be ye sorry; for the joy of the Lord is your strength.   ❦ *Nehemiah 8:10*

And thou shalt rejoice in the Lord, and shalt glory in the Holy One of Israel.   ❦ *Isaiah 41:16*

The righteous shall be glad in the Lord, and shall trust in him; and all the upright in heart shall glory.
                                        ❦ *Psalm 64:10*

My soul shall be satisfied as with marrow and fatness; and my mouth shall praise thee with joyful lips.
                                        ❦ *Psalm 63:5*

But let the righteous be glad; let them rejoice before God: yea, let them exceedingly rejoice.   ❦ *Psalm 68:3*

I will see you again, and your heart shall rejoice, and your joy no man taketh from you.   ❦ *John 16:22*

Laziness

And that ye study to be quiet, and to do your own business, and to work with your own hands, as we commanded you;

That ye may walk honestly toward them that are without, and that ye may have lack of nothing.

❦ *1 Thessalonians 4:11–12*

Not slothful in business; fervent in spirit; serving the Lord. ❦ *Romans 12:11*

He that tilleth his land shall have plenty of bread: but he that followeth after vain persons shall have poverty enough. ❦ *Proverbs 28:19*

The soul of the sluggard desireth, and hath nothing: but the soul of the diligent shall be made fat.

❦ *Proverbs 13:4*

He becometh poor that dealeth with a slack hand: but the hand of the diligent maketh rich.

He that gathereth in summer is a wise son: but he that sleepeth in harvest is a son that causeth shame.

❦ *Proverbs 10:4–5*

Much food is in the tillage of the poor: but there is that is destroyed for want of judgment. ❦ *Proverbs 13:23*

The husbandman that laboureth must be first partaker of the fruits. ❦ *2 Timothy 2:6*

For even when we were with you, this we commanded you, that if any would not work, neither should he eat.

For we hear that there are some which walk among you disorderly, working not at all, but are busybodies.

Now them that are such we command and exhort by our Lord Jesus Christ, that with quietness they work, and eat their own bread.   ❦ *2 Thessalonians 3:10–12*

I went by the field of the slothful, and by the vineyard of the man void of understanding;

And, lo, it was all grown over with thorns, and nettles had covered the face thereof, and the stone wall thereof was broken down.

Then I saw, and considered it well: I looked upon it, and received instruction.

Yet a little sleep, a little slumber, a little folding of the hands to sleep:

So shall thy poverty come as one that travelleth; and thy want as an armed man.   ❦ *Proverbs 24:30–34*

Love not sleep, lest thou come to poverty; open thine eyes, and thou shalt be satisfied with bread.
                                                   ❦ *Proverbs 20:13*

The way of the slothful man is as an hedge of thorns: but the way of the righteous is made plain.
                                                   ❦ *Proverbs 15:19*

Be thou diligent to know the state of thy flocks, and look well to thy herds.   ❦ *Proverbs 27:23*

The thoughts of the diligent tend only to plenteousness; but of every one that is hasty only to want.

❦ *Proverbs 21:5*

The hand of the diligent shall bear rule: but the slothful shall be under tribute. ❦ *Proverbs 12:24*

Let him that stole steal no more: but rather let him labour, working with his hands the thing which is good, that he may have to give to him that needeth.

❦ *Ephesians 4:28*

He that tilleth his land shall be satisfied with bread: but he that followeth vain persons is void of understanding.

❦ *Proverbs 12:11*

And thou shalt have goats' milk enough for thy food, for the food of thy household, and for the maintenance for thy maidens. ❦ *Proverbs 27:27*

Behold that which I have seen: it is good and comely for one to eat and drink, and to enjoy the good of all his labour that he taketh under the sun all the days of his life, which God giveth him: for it is his portion.

Every man also to whom God hath given riches and wealth, and hath given him power to eat thereof, and to take his portion, and to rejoice in his labour; this is the gift of God. ❦ *Ecclesiastes 5:18–19*

Loneliness

I will not leave you comfortless: I will come to you.

❧ *John 14:18*

Then shalt thou call, and the Lord shall answer; thou shalt cry, and he shall say, Here I am.

❧ *Isaiah 58:9*

Since thou wast precious in my sight, thou hast been honourable, and I have loved thee.

❧ *Isaiah 43:4*

And will be a Father unto you, and ye shall be my sons and daughters, saith the Lord Almighty.

❧ *2 Corinthians 6:18*

And, behold, I am with thee, and will keep thee in all places whither thou goest, and will bring thee again into this land; for I will not leave thee, until I have done that which I have spoken to thee of.

❧ *Genesis 28:15*

And ye are complete in him, which is the the head of all principality and power. ❧ *Colossians 2:10*

But I am poor and needy; yet the Lord thinketh upon me: thou art my help and my deliverer; make no tarrying, O my God. ❧ *Psalm 40:17*

Long Life

And even to your old age I am he; and even to hoar hairs will I carry you: I have made, and I will bear; even I will carry, and will deliver you. ❦ *Isaiah 46:4*

With the ancient is wisdom; and in length of days understanding.

With him is wisdom and strength, he hath counsel and understanding. ❦ *Job 12:12–13*

The glory of young men is their strength: and the beauty of old men is the grey head. ❦ *Proverbs 20:29*

Children's children are the crown of old men; and the glory of children are their fathers. ❦ *Proverbs 17:6*

Thou shalt come to thy grave in a full age, like as a shock of corn cometh in in his season. ❦ *Job 5:26*

And thine age shall be clearer than the noonday; thou shalt shine forth, thou shalt be as the morning.

❦ *Job 11:17*

My son, forget not my law; but let thine heart keep my commandments:

For length of days, and long life, and peace, shall they add to thee. ❦ *Proverbs 3:1–2*

Cast me not off in the time of old age; forsake me not when my strength faileth. ❦ *Psalm 71:9*

But speak thou the things which become sound doctrine:

That the aged men be sober, grave, temperate, sound in faith, in charity, in patience.

The aged women likewise, that they be in behaviour as becometh holiness, not false accusers, not given to much wine, teachers of good things;

That they may teach the young women to be sober, to love their husbands, to love their children,

To be discreet, chaste, keepers at home, good, obedient to their own husbands, that the word of God be not blasphemed. ❦ *Titus 2:1–5*

O God, thou hast taught me from my youth: and hitherto have I declared thy wondrous works.

Now also when I am old and greyheaded, O God, forsake me not; until I have shewed thy strength unto this generation, and thy power to every one that is to come.
❦ *Psalm 71:17–18*

Lord, make me to know mine end, and the measure of my days, what it is; that I may know how frail I am.

Behold, thou hast made my days as an handbreadth; and mine age is as nothing before thee.
❦ *Psalm 39:4–5*

Ye shall walk in all the ways which the Lord your God hath commanded you, that ye may live, and that it may be well with you, and that ye may prolong your days in the land ye shall possess. ❦ *Deuteronomy 5:33*

With long life will I satisfy him, and shew him my salvation. ❦ *Psalm 91:16*

That thou mightest fear the Lord thy God, to keep all his statutes and his commandments, which I command thee, thou, and thy son, and thy son's son, all the days of thy life; and that thy days may be prolonged.

❧ *Deuteronomy 6:2*

The fear of the Lord prolongeth days: but the years of the wicked shall be shortened. ❧ *Proverbs 10:27*

For by me thy days shall be multiplied, and the years of thy life shall be increased. ❧ *Proverbs 9:11*

Love, Brotherly

A new commandment I give unto you, That ye love one another; as I have loved you, that ye also love one another.

By this shall all men know that ye are my disciples, if ye have love one to another.   ❦ *John 13:34–35*

Let love be without dissimulation. Abhor that which is evil; cleave to that which is good.

Be kindly affectioned one to another with brotherly love; in honour preferring one another.

❦ *Romans 12:9–10*

But as touching brotherly love ye need not that I write unto you: for ye yourselves are taught of God to love one another.   ❦ *1 Thessalonians 4:9*

He that loveth his brother abideth in the light, and there is none occasion of stumbling in him.   ❦ *1 John 2:10*

Seeing ye have purified your souls in obeying the truth through the Spirit unto unfeigned love of the brethren, see that ye love one another with a pure heart fervently.

❦ *1 Peter 1:22*

My little children, let us not love in word, neither in tongue; but in deed and in truth.   ❦ *1 John 3:18*

Beloved, if God so loved us, we ought also to love one another.   ❦ *1 John 4:11*

Beloved, let us loved one another: for love is of God; and every one that loveth is born of God, and knoweth God.

He that loveth not knoweth not God; for God is love.
🦃 *1 John 4:7–8*

Put on therefore, as the elect of God, holy and beloved, bowels of mercies, kindness, humbleness of mind, meekness, longsuffering;

Forbearing one another, and forgiving one another, if any man have a quarrel against any: even as Christ forgave you, so also do ye.　　🦃 *Colossians 3:12–13*

Love, God's

For God so loved the world, that he gave his only begotten Son, that whosoever believeth in him should not perish, but have everlasting life. ❦ *John 3:16*

And he will love thee, and bless thee, and multiply thee: he will also bless the fruit of thy womb, and the fruit of thy land, thy corn, and thy wine, and thine oil, the increase of thy kine, and the flocks of thy sheep, in the land which he sware unto thy fathers to give thee.
❦ *Deuteronomy 7:13*

The Lord openeth the eyes of the blind: the Lord raiseth them that are bowed down: the Lord loveth the righteous.
❦ *Psalm 146:8*

The way of the wicked is an abomination unto the Lord: but he loveth him that followeth after righteousness.
❦ *Proverbs 15:9*

For as a young man marrieth a virgin, so shall thy sons marry thee: and as the bridegroom rejoiceth over the bride, so shall thy God rejoice over thee.
❦ *Isaiah 62:5*

Herein is love, not that we loved God, but that he loved us, and sent his Son to be the propitiation for our sins.
❦ *1 John 4:10*

I will heal their backsliding, I will love them freely: for mine anger is turned away from him.   ❦ *Hosea 14:4*

The Lord thy God in the midst of thee is mighty; he will save, he will rejoice over thee with joy; he will rest in his love, he will joy over thee with singing.

❦ *Zephaniah 3:17*

The Lord hath appeared of old unto me, saying, Yea, I have loved thee with an everlasting love: therefore with lovingkindness have I drawn thee.   ❦ *Jeremiah 31:3*

Yea, I will rejoice over them to do them good, and I will plant them in this land assuredly with my whole heart and with my whole soul.   ❦ *Jeremiah 32:41*

But God, who is rich in mercy, for his great love wherewith he loved us,

Even when we were dead in sins, hath quickened us together with Christ, (by grace ye are saved;)

And hath raised us up together, and made us sit together in heavenly places in Christ Jesus:

That in the ages to come he might shew the exceeding riches of his grace in his kindness toward us through Christ Jesus.   ❦ *Ephesians 2:4–7*

And we have known and believed the love that God hath to us. God is love; and he that dwelleth in love dwelleth in God, and God in him.   ❦ *1 John 4:16*

For the Father himself loveth you, because ye have loved
me, and have believed that I came out from God.

❦ *John 16:27*

We love him, because he first loved us.

❦ *1 John 4:19*

And I have declared unto them thy name, and will
declare it: that the love wherewith thou hast loved me
may be in them, and I in them.   ❦ *John 17:26*

I in them, and thou in me, that they may be made perfect
in one; and that the world may know that thou hast sent
me, and hast loved them, as thou hast loved me.

❦ *John 17:23*

Now our Lord Jesus Christ himself, and God, even our
Father, which hath loved us, and hath given us everlasting consolation and good hope through grace,

   Comfort your hearts, and stablish you in every good
word and work.   ❦ *2 Thessalonians 2:16–17*

Loving God

Know therefore that the Lord thy God, he is God, the faithful God, which keepeth covenant and mercy with them that love him and keep his commandments to a thousand generations. ❧ *Deuteronomy 7:9*

I love them that love me; and those that seek me early shall find me. ❧ *Proverbs 8:17*

He that hath my commandments, and keepeth them, he it is that loveth me: and he that loveth me shall be loved of my Father, and I will love him, and will manifest myself to him. ❧ *John 14:21*

That I may cause those that love me to inherit substance; and I will fill their treasures. ❧ *Proverbs 8:21*

Delight thyself also in the Lord; and he shall give thee the desires of thine heart. ❧ *Psalm 37:4*

Because he hath set his love upon me, therefore will I deliver him: I will set him on high, because he hath known my name. ❧ *Psalm 91:14*

But as it is written, Eye hath not seen, nor ear heard, neither have entered into the heart of man, the things which God hath prepared for them that love him.
❧ *1 Corinthians 2:9*

The Lord preserveth all them that love him: but all the wicked will he destroy. ❦ *Psalm 145:20*

And it shall come to pass, if ye shall hearken diligently unto my commandments which I command you this day, to love the Lord your God, and to serve him with all your heart and with all your soul,

That I will give you the rain of your land in his due season, the first rain and the latter rain, that thou mayest gather in thy corn, and thy wine, and thine oil.

And I will send grass in thy fields for thy cattle, that thou mayest eat and be full.

❦ *Deuteronomy 11:13–15*

Grace be with all them that love our Lord Jesus Christ in sincerity. Amen. ❦ *Ephesians 6:24*

Lust

From whence come wars and fightings among you? come they not hence, even of your lusts that war in your members?

Ye lust, and have not: ye kill, and desire to have, and cannot obtain: ye fight and war, yet ye have not, because ye ask not.

Ye ask, and receive not, because ye ask amiss, that ye may consume it upon your lusts.

Ye adulterers and adulteresses, know ye not that the friendship of the world is enmity with God? whosoever therefore will be a friend of the world is the enemy of God.   ❦ *James 4:1–4*

For all that is in the world, the lust of the flesh, and the lust of the eyes, and the pride of life, is not of the Father, but is of the world.

And the world passeth away, and the lust thereof: but he that doeth the will of God abideth for ever.

❦ *1 John 2:16–17*

Ye have heard that it was said by them of old time, Thou shalt not commit adultery:

But I say unto you, That whosoever looketh on a woman to lust after her hath committed adultery with her already in his heart.   ❦ *Matthew 5:27–28*

Lust not after her beauty in thine heart; neither let her take thee with her eyelids.

For by means of a whorish woman a man is brought

to a piece of bread: and the adulteress will hunt for the precious life.

Can a man take fire in his bosom, and his clothes not be burned?

Can one go upon hot coals, and his feet not be burned?

So he that goeth in to his neighbour's wife; whosoever toucheth her shall not be innocent.

❦ *Proverbs 6:25–29*

Submit yourselves therefore to God. Resist the devil, and he will flee from you.

Draw nigh to God, and he will draw nigh to you. Cleanse your hands, ye sinners; and purify your hearts, ye double minded. ❦ *James 4:7–8*

Dearly beloved, I beseech you as strangers and pilgrims, abstain from fleshly lusts, which war against the soul. ❦ *1 Peter 2:11*

As obedient children, not fashioning yourselves according to the former lusts in your ignorance:

But as he which hath called you is holy, so be ye holy in all manner of conversation;

Because it is written, Be ye holy; for I am holy.

❦ *1 Peter 1:14–16*

Whereby are given unto us exceeding great and precious promises: that by these ye might be partakers of the divine nature, having escaped the corruption that is in the world through lust. ❦ *2 Peter 1:4*

And they that are Christ's have crucified the flesh with the affections and lusts. ❦ *Galatians 5:24*

Flee also youthful lusts: but follow righteousness, faith, charity, peace, with them that call on the Lord out of a pure heart. ❦ *2 Timothy 2:22*

For we ourselves also were sometimes foolish, disobedient, deceived, serving divers lusts and pleasures, living in malice and envy, hateful, and hating one another.

But after that the kindness and love of God our Saviour toward man appeared,

Not by works of righteousness which we have done, but according to his mercy he saved us, by the washing of regeneration, and renewing of the Holy Ghost.

❦ *Titus 3:3–5*

We all had our conversation in times past in the lusts of our flesh, fulfilling the desires of the flesh and of the mind; and were by nature the children of wrath, even as others.

But God, who is rich in mercy, for his great love wherewith he loved us,

Even when we were dead in sins, hath quickened us together with Christ, (by grace ye are saved;)

And hath raised us up together, and made us sit together in heavenly places in Christ Jesus.

❦ *Ephesians 2:3–6*

For the grace of God that bringeth salvation hath appeared to all men,

Teaching us that, denying ungodliness and worldly lusts, we should live soberly, righteously, and godly, in this present world. ❦ *Titus 2:11–12*

They told you there should be mockers in the last time, who should walk after their own ungodly lusts.

These be they who separate themselves, sensual, having not the Spirit.

But ye, beloved, building up yourselves on your most holy faith, praying in the Holy Ghost,

Keep yourselves in the love of God, looking for the mercy of our Lord Jesus Christ unto eternal life.

❦ *Jude 18–21*

Walk in the Spirit, and ye shall not fulfil the lust of the flesh.

For the flesh lusteth against the Spirit, and the Spirit against the flesh: and these are contrary the one to the other: so that ye cannot do the things that ye would.

❦ *Galatians 5:16–17*

Likewise reckon ye also yourselves to be dead indeed unto sin, but alive unto God through Jesus Christ our Lord.

Let not sin therefore reign in your mortal body, that ye should obey it in the lusts thereof.

For sin shall not have dominion over you: for ye are not under the law, but under grace.

❦ *Romans 6:11–12, 14*

But put ye on the Lord Jesus Christ, and make not provision for the flesh, to fulfil the lusts thereof.

❦ *Romans 13:14*

Lying

Lie not one to another, seeing that ye have put off the old man with his deeds;

And have put on the new man, which is renewed in knowledge after the image of him that created him.

❦ *Colossians 3:9–10*

And ye shall not swear by my name falsely, neither shalt thou profane the name of thy God: I am the Lord.

❦ *Leviticus 19:12*

A man that beareth false witness against his neighbour is a maul, and a sword, and a sharp arrow.

❦ *Proverbs 25:18*

A faithful witness will not lie: but a false witness will utter lies.

❦ *Proverbs 14:5*

Thou shalt not raise a false report: put not thine hand with the wicked to be an unrighteous witness.

❦ *Exodus 23:1*

A false witness shall not be unpunished, and he that speaketh lies shall not escape.

❦ *Proverbs 19:5*

But the fearful, and unbelieving, and the abominable, and murderers, and whoremongers, and sorcerers, and idolaters, and all liars, shall have their part in the lake which burneth with fire and brimstone: which is the second death.

❦ *Revelation 21:8*

If a false witness rise up against any man to testify against him that which is wrong;

Then both the men, between whom the controversy is, shall stand before the Lord, before the priests and the judges, which shall be in those days;

And the judges shall make diligent inquisition: and, behold, if the witness be a false witness, and hath testified falsely against his brother;

Then shall ye do unto him, as he had thought to have done unto his brother: so shalt thou put the evil away from among you.   ❦ *Deuteronomy 19:16–19*

A false witness shall not be unpunished, and he that speaketh lies shall perish.   ❦ *Proverbs 19:9*

Be not a witness against thy neighbour without cause; and deceive not with thy lips.   ❦ *Proverbs 24:28*

The wicked are estranged from the womb: they go astray as soon as they be born, speaking lies.   ❦ *Psalm 58:3*

But if ye have bitter envying and strife in your hearts, glory not, and lie not against the truth.   ❦ *James 3:14*

The lip of truth shall be established for ever: but a lying tongue is but for a moment.   ❦ *Proverbs 12:19*

Marriage

Live joyfully with the wife whom thou lovest all the days of the life of thy vanity, which he hath given thee under the sun, all the days of thy vanity: for that is thy portion in this life, and in thy labour which thou takest under the sun.

❧ Ecclesiastes 9:9

Drink waters out of thine own cistern, and running waters out of thine own well. *❧ Proverbs 5:15*

Let thy fountain be blessed: and rejoice with the wife of thy youth.

Let her be as the loving hind and pleasant roe; let her breasts satisfy thee at all times; and be thou ravished always with her love.

And why wilt thou, my son, be ravished with a strange woman, and embrace the bosom of a stranger?

❧ Proverbs 5:18–20

Let the husband render unto the wife due benevolence: and likewise also the wife unto the husband.

❧ 1 Corinthians 7:3

Wives, submit yourselves unto your own husbands, as unto the Lord.

For the husband is the head of the wife, even as Christ is the head of the church: and he is the saviour of the body. *❧ Ephesians 5:22–23*

Husbands, love your wives, even as Christ also loved the church, and gave himself for it.

Ephesians 5:25

So ought men to love their wives as their own bodies. He that loveth his wife loveth himself.

Ephesians 5:28

For this cause shall a man leave his father and mother, and shall be joined unto his wife, and they two shall be one flesh.

Ephesians 5:31

Nevertheless let every one of you in particular so love his wife even as himself; and the wife see that she reverence her husband.

Ephesians 5:33

But if any provide not for his own, and specially for those of his own house, he hath denied the faith, and is worse than an infidel.

1 Timothy 5:8

Wives submit yourselves unto your own husbands, as it is fit in the Lord.

Husbands, love your wives, and be not bitter against them.

Colossians 3:18–19

Likewise, ye husbands, dwell with them according to knowledge, giving honour unto the wife, as unto the weaker vessel, and as being heirs together of the grace of life; that your prayers be not hindered.

1 Peter 3:7

That they may teach the young women to be sober, to love their husbands, to love their children,

To be discreet, chaste, keepers at home, good, obedient to their own husbands, that the word of God be not blasphemed. ❧ *Titus 2:4–5*

Meekness

Blessed are the meek: for they shall inherit the earth.

❦ Matthew 5:5

But with righteousness shall he judge the poor, and reprove with equity for the meek of the earth.

❦ Isaiah 11:4

The meek also shall increase their joy in the Lord, and the poor among men shall rejoice in the Holy One of Israel.

❦ Isaiah 29:19

The Lord lifteth up the meek: he casteth the wicked down to the ground.

❦ Psalm 147:6

The meek will he guide in judgment: and the meek will he teach his way.

❦ Psalm 25:9

But the meek shall inherit the earth; and shall delight themselves in the abundance of peace.

❦ Psalm 37:11

A soft answer turneth away wrath: but grievous words stir up anger.

❦ Proverbs 15:1

Seek ye the Lord, all ye meek of the earth, which have wrought his judgment; seek righteousness, seek meekness: it may be ye shall be hid in the day of the Lord's anger.

❦ Zephaniah 2:3

But let it be the hidden man of the heart, in that which is not corruptible, even the ornament of a meek and quiet spirit, which is in the sight of God of great price.

❦ *1 Peter 3:4*

The meek shall eat and be satisfied: they shall praise the Lord that seek him: your heart shall live for ever.

❦ *Psalm 22:26*

For the Lord taketh pleasure in his people: he will beautify the meek with salvation. ❦ *Psalm 149:4*

Mercy

And therefore will the Lord wait, that he may be gracious unto you, and therefore will he be exalted, that he may have mercy upon you: for the Lord is a God of judgment: blessed are all they that wait for him.

❦ *Isaiah 30:18*

Know therefore that God exacteth of thee less than thine iniquity deserveth. ❦ *Job 11:6*

Like as a father pitieth his children, so the Lord pitieth them that fear him. ❦ *Psalm 103:13*

But the mercy of the Lord is from everlasting to everlasting upon them that fear him, and his righteousness unto children's children. ❦ *Psalm 103:17*

And he said, I will make all my goodness pass before thee, and I will proclaim the name of the Lord before thee; and will be gracious to whom I will be gracious, and will shew mercy on whom I will shew mercy.

❦ *Exodus 33:19*

And I will have mercy upon her that had not obtained mercy; and I will say to them which were not my people, Thou art my people; and they shall say, Thou art my God.

❦ *Hosea 2:23*

For in my wrath I smote thee, but in my favour have I had mercy on thee. ❦ *Isaiah 60:10*

For my name's sake will I defer mine anger, and for my praise will I refrain for thee, that I cut thee not off.

❦ *Isaiah 48:9*

Money

Labour not to be rich: cease from thine own wisdom.

Wilt thou set thine eyes upon that which is not? for riches certainly make themselves wings; they fly away as an eagle toward heaven. ❦ *Proverbs 23:4–5*

A little that a righteous man hath is better than the riches of many wicked. ❦ *Psalm 37:16*

Hearken, my beloved brethren, Hath not God chosen the poor of this world rich in faith, and heirs of the kingdom which he hath promised to them that love him?
❦ *James 2:5*

Better is an handful with quietness, than both the hands full with travail and vexation of spirit.
❦ *Ecclesiastes 4:6*

For the oppression of the poor, for the sighing of the needy, now will I arise, saith the Lord; I will set him in safety from him that puffeth at him. ❦ *Psalm 12:5*

Whoso mocketh the poor reproacheth his Maker: and he that is glad at calamities shall not be unpunished.
❦ *Proverbs 17:5*

But he saveth the poor from the sword, from their mouth, and from the hand of the mighty.

So the poor hath hope, and iniquity stoppeth her mouth. ❦ *Job 5:15–16*

Rob not the poor, because he is poor: neither oppress the afflicted in the gate.   ❦ *Proverbs 22:22*

Charge them that are rich in this world, that they be not highminded, nor trust in uncertain riches, but in the living God, who giveth us richly all things to enjoy;

    That they do good, that they be rich in good works, ready to distribute, willing to communicate;

    Laying up in store for themselves a good foundation against the time to come, that they may lay hold on eternal life.   ❦ *1 Timothy 6:17–19*

The sleep of a labouring man is sweet, whether he eat little or much: but the abundance of the rich will not suffer him to sleep.

    There is a sore evil which I have seen under the sun, namely, riches kept for the owners thereof to their hurt.

    But those riches perish by evil travail: and be begetteth a son, and there is nothing in his hand.

     ❦ *Ecclesiastes 5:12–14*

But thou shalt remember the Lord thy God: for it is he that giveth thee power to get wealth, that he may establish his covenant which he sware unto thy fathers, as it is this day.   ❦ *Deuteronomy 8:18*

Better is little with the fear of the Lord than great treasure and trouble therewith.   ❦ *Proverbs 15:16*

The rich and poor meet together: the Lord is the maker of them all.   ❦ *Proverbs 22:2*

For the needy shall not alway be forgotten: the expectation of the poor shall not perish for ever.

🐦 *Psalm 9:18*

He that trusteth in his riches shall fall: but the righteous shall flourish as a branch. 🐦 *Proverbs 11:28*

A faithful man shall abound with blessings: but he that maketh haste to be rich shall not be innocent.

🐦 *Proverbs 28:20*

Riches profit not in the day of wrath: but righteousness delivereth from death. 🐦 *Proverbs 11:4*

They shall cast their silver in the streets, and their gold shall be removed: their silver and their gold shall not be able to deliver them in the day of the wrath of the Lord: they shall not satisfy their souls, neither fill their bowels: because it is the stumblingblock of their iniquity.

🐦 *Ezekiel 7:19*

There is that maketh himself rich, yet hath nothing: there is that maketh himself poor, yet hath great riches.

🐦 *Proverbs 13:7*

He that loveth silver shall not be satisfied with silver; nor he that loveth abundance with increase: this is also vanity.

🐦 *Ecclesiastes 5:10*

He that oppresseth the poor to increase his riches, and he that giveth to the rich, shall surely come to want.

🐦 *Proverbs 22:16*

He that hasteth to be rich hath an evil eye, and considereth not that poverty shall come upon him.

❦ Proverbs 28:22

He delivereth the poor in his affliction, and openeth their ears in oppression. *❦ Job 36:15*

Better is the poor that walketh in his uprightness, than he that is perverse in his ways, though he be rich.

❦ Proverbs 28:6

Blessed is he that considereth the poor: the Lord will deliver him in time of trouble. *❦ Psalm 41:1*

Obedience

See, I have set before thee this day life and good, and death and evil;

In that I command thee this day to love the Lord thy God, to walk in his ways, and to keep his commandments and his statutes and his judgments, that thou mayest live and multiply: and the Lord thy God shall bless thee in the land whither thou goest to possess it.

❦ *Deuteronomy 30:15–16*

And thou shalt do that which is right and good in the sight of the Lord: that it may be well with thee, and that thou mayest go in and possess the good land which the Lord sware unto thy fathers. ❦ *Deuteronomy 6:18*

Hear therefore, O Israel, and observe to do it; that it may be well with thee, and that ye may increase mightily, as the Lord God of thy fathers hath promised thee, in the land that floweth with milk and honey.

❦ *Deuteronomy 6:3*

Wherefore it shall come to pass, if ye hearken to these judgments, and keep, and do them, that the Lord thy God shall keep unto thee the covenant and the mercy which he sware unto thy fathers. ❦ *Deuteronomy 7:12*

Keep therefore the words of this covenant, and do them, that ye may prosper in all that ye do.

❦ *Deuteronomy 29:9*

O that there were such an heart in them, that they would fear me, and keep all my commandments always, that it might be well with them, and with their children for ever!
 ❦ *Deuteronomy 5:29*

Those things, which ye have both learned, and received, and heard, and seen in me, do: and the God of peace shall be with you. ❦ *Philippians 4:9*

Whosoever therefore shall break one of these least commandments, and shall teach men so, he shall be called the least in the kingdom of heaven: but whosoever shall do and teach them, the same shall be called great in the kingdom of heaven. ❦ *Matthew 5:19*

Therefore whosoever heareth these sayings of mine, and doeth them, I will liken him unto a wise man, which built his house upon a rock:

And the rain descended, and the floods came, and the winds blew, and beat upon that house; and it fell not: for it was founded upon a rock. ❦ *Matthew 7:24–25*

If they obey and serve him, they shall spend their days in prosperity, and their years in pleasures. ❦ *Job 36:11*

And we know that all things work together for good to them that love God, to them who are the called according to his purpose. ❦ *Romans 8:28*

If ye know these things, happy are ye if ye do them.
 ❦ *John 13:17*

If ye keep my commandments, ye shall abide in my love; even as I have kept my Father's commandments, and abide in his love. 🐚 *John 15:10*

But whoso looketh into the perfect law of liberty, and continueth therein, he being not a forgetful hearer, but a doer of the work, this man shall be blessed in his deed.
🐚 *James 1:25*

For not the hearers of the law are just before God, but the doers of the law shall be justified.
🐚 *Romans 2:13*

Verily, verily, I say unto you, He that heareth my word, and believeth on him that sent me, hath everlasting life, and shall not come into condemnation; but is passed from death unto life. 🐚 *John 5:24*

For whosoever shall do the will of my Father which is in heaven, the same is my brother, and sister, and mother.
🐚 *Matthew 12:50*

And the world passeth away, and the lust thereof: but he that doeth the will of God abideth for ever.
🐚 *1 John 2:17*

Not every one that saith unto me, Lord, Lord, shall enter into the kingdom of heaven; but he that doeth the will of my Father which is in heaven. 🐚 *Matthew 7:21*

And whatsoever we ask, we receive of him, because we keep his commandments, and do those things that are pleasing in his sight. ❦ *1 John 3:22*

Parents' Duties

For I know him, that he will command his children and his household after him, and they shall keep the way of the Lord, to do justice and judgment.

❦ *Genesis 18:19*

Shewing to the generation to come the praises of the Lord, and his strength, and his wonderful works that he hath done.

For he established a testimony in Jacob, and appointed a law in Israel, which he commanded our fathers, that they should make them known to their children:

That the generation to come might know them, even the children which should be born; who should arise and declare them to their children:

That they might set their hope in God, and not forget the works of God, but keep his commandments.

❦ *Psalm 78:4–7*

And thou shalt shew thy son in that day, saying, This is done because of that which the Lord did unto me when I came forth out of Egypt. ❦ *Exodus 13:8*

And, ye fathers, provoke not your children to wrath: but bring them up in the nurture and admonition of the Lord.

❦ *Ephesians 6:4*

Fathers, provoke not your children to anger, lest they be discouraged. ❦ *Colossians 3:21*

Only take heed to thyself, and keep thy soul diligently, lest thou forget the things which thine eyes have seen, and lest they depart from thy heart all the days of thy life: but teach them thy sons, and thy sons' sons; . . .

Gather me the people together, and I will make them hear my words, that they may learn to fear me all the days that they shall live upon the earth, and that they may teach their children. ❦ *Deuteronomy 4:9–10*

Train up a child in the way he should go: and when he old, he will not depart from it. ❦ *Proverbs 22:6*

And ye shall teach them your children, speaking of them when thou sittest in thine house, and when thou walkest by the way, when thou liest down, and when thou risest up.
❦ *Deuteronomy 11:19*

Correct thy son, and he shall give thee rest; yea, he shall give delight unto thy soul. ❦ *Proverbs 29:17*

Patience

Be patient therefore, brethren, unto the coming of the Lord. Behold, the husbandman waiteth for the precious fruit of the earth, and hath long patience for it, until he receive the early and latter rain.

Be ye also patient; stablish your hearts: for the coming of the Lord draweth nigh. ❦ *James 5:7–8*

For what glory is it, if, when ye be buffeted for your faults, ye shall take it patiently? but if, when ye do well, and suffer for it, ye take it patiently, this is acceptable with God. ❦ *1 Peter 2:20*

And let us not be weary in well doing: for in due season we shall reap, if we faint not. ❦ *Galatians 6:9*

Let us hold fast the profession of our faith without wavering; (for he is faithful that promised).
❦ *Hebrews 10:23*

But he that shall endure unto the end, the same shall be saved. ❦ *Matthew 24:13*

That ye be not slothful, but followers of them who through faith and patience inherit the promises.
❦ *Hebrews 6:12*

For ye have need of patience, that, after ye have done the will of God, ye might receive the promise.
❦ *Hebrews 10:36*

My brethren, count it all joy when ye fall into divers temptations;

Knowing this, that the trying of your faith worketh patience.

But let patience have her perfect work, that ye may be perfect and entire, wanting nothing.

❦ *James 1:2–4*

And not only so, but we glory in tribulations also: knowing that tribulation worketh patience;

And patience, experience, and experience, hope.

❦ *Romans 5:3–4*

Peace

Peace, peace to him that is far off, and to him that is near, saith the Lord; and I will heal him.

❦ Isaiah 57:19

And let the peace of God rule in your hearts, to the which also ye are called in one body; and be ye thankful.

❦ Colossians 3:15

I will hear what God the Lord will speak: for he will speak peace unto his people, and to his saints.

❦ Psalm 85:8

And the peace of God, which passeth all understanding, shall keep your hearts and minds through Christ Jesus.

❦ Philippians 4:7

And the work of righteousness shall be peace; and the effect of righteousness quietness and assurance for ever.

❦ Isaiah 32:17

Thy faith hath saved thee; go in peace.

❦ Luke 7:50

Mark the perfect man, and behold the upright: for the end of that man is peace.   *❦ Psalm 37:37*

Now the Lord of peace himself give you peace always by all means.   *❦ 2 Thessalonians 3:16*

Peace I leave with you, my peace I give unto you: not as the world giveth, give I unto you. Let not your heart be troubled, neither let it be afraid.   ❦ *John 14:27*

Poverty

For he shall deliver the needy when he crieth; the poor also, and him that hath no helper.

He shall spare the poor and needy, and shall save the souls of the needy. ❦ *Psalm 72:12–13*

Yet setteth he the poor on high from affliction, and maketh him families like a flock. ❦ *Psalm 107:41*

For the Lord heareth the poor, and despiseth not his prisoners. ❦ *Psalm 69:33*

Sing unto the Lord, praise ye the Lord: for he hath delivered the soul of the poor from the hand of evildoers.

❦ *Jeremiah 20:13*

He will regard the prayer of the destitute, and not despise their prayer. ❦ *Psalm 102:17*

He raiseth up the poor out of the dust, and lifteth the needy out of the dunghill. ❦ *Psalm 113:7*

I will abundantly bless her provision: I will satisfy her poor with bread. ❦ *Psalm 132:15*

Thou, O God, hast prepared of thy goodness for the poor.

❦ *Psalm 68:10*

Prayer

Ask, and it shall be given you; seek, and ye shall find; knock, and it shall be opened unto you:

For every one that asketh receiveth; and he that seeketh findeth; and to him that knocketh it shall be opened. ❧ *Matthew 7:7–8*

And all things, whatsoever ye shall ask in prayer, believing, ye shall receive. ❧ *Matthew 21:22*

He will be very gracious unto thee at the voice of thy cry; when he shall hear it, he will answer thee.

❧ *Isaiah 30:19*

And this is the confidence that we have in him, that, if we ask any thing according to his will, he heareth us:

And if we know that he hear us, whatsoever we ask, we know that we have the petitions that we desired of him. ❧ *1 John 5:14–15*

And it shall come to pass, that before they call, I will answer; and while they are yet speaking, I will hear.

❧ *Isaiah 65:24*

Whatsoever ye shall ask the Father in my name, he will give it you.

Hitherto have ye asked nothing in my name: ask, and ye shall receive, that your joy may be full.

❧ *John 16:23–24*

Confess your faults one to another, and pray one for another, that ye may be healed. The effectual fervent prayer of a righteous man availeth much.

❦ *James 5:16*

Thou shalt make thy prayer unto him, and he shall hear thee. ❦ *Job 22:27*

And whatsoever ye shall ask in my name, that will I do, that the Father may be glorified in the Son.

If ye shall ask any thing in my name, I will do it.

❦ *John 14:13–14*

If ye abide in me, and my words abide in you, ye shall ask what ye will, and it shall be done unto you.

❦ *John 15:7*

But thou, when thou prayest, enter into thy closet, and when thou hast shut thy door, pray to thy Father which is in secret; and thy Father which seeth in secret shall reward thee openly. ❦ *Matthew 6:6*

He shall call upon me, and I will answer him.

❦ *Psalm 91:15*

The Lord is far from the wicked: but he heareth the prayer of the righteous. ❦ *Proverbs 15:29*

O thou that hearest prayer, unto thee shall all flesh come.

❦ *Psalm 65:2*

The righteous cry, and the Lord heareth, and delivereth them out of all their troubles. ❦ *Psalm 34:17*

If ye then, being evil, know how to give good gifts unto your children, how much more shall your Father which is in heaven give good things to them that ask him?
❦ *Matthew 7:11*

Then shalt thou call, and the Lord shall answer; thou shalt cry, and he shall say, Here I am.
❦ *Isaiah 58:9*

Evening, and morning, and at noon, will I pray, and cry aloud: and he shall hear my voice. ❦ *Psalm 55:17*

The Lord is nigh unto all them that call upon him, to all that call upon him in truth.

He will fulfil the desire of them that fear him: he also will hear their cry, and will save them.
❦ *Psalm 145:18–19*

And I will bring the third part through the fire, and will refine them as silver is refined, and will try them as gold is tried: they shall call on my name, and I will hear them: I will say, It is my people: and they shall say, the Lord is my God. ❦ *Zechariah 13:9*

Be not ye therefore like unto them: for your Father knoweth what things ye have need of, before ye ask him.
❦ *Matthew 6:8*

Then shall ye call upon me, and ye shall go and pray unto me, and I will hearken unto you.   ❦ *Jeremiah 29:12*

And whatsoever we ask, we receive of him, because we keep his commandments, and do those things that are pleasing in his sight.   ❦ *1 John 3:22*

Pride

Pride goeth before destruction, and an haughty spirit before a fall. *Proverbs 16:18*

Woe unto them that are wise in their own eyes, and prudent in their own sight! *Isaiah 5:21*

Seest thou a man wise in his own conceit? there is more hope of a fool than of him. *Proverbs 26:12*

Look on every one that is proud, and bring him low; and tread down the wicked in their place. *Job 40:12*

An high look, and a proud heart, and the plowing of the wicked, is sin. *Proverbs 21:4*

The fear of the Lord is to hate evil: pride, and arrogancy, and the evil way, and the froward mouth, do I hate. *Proverbs 8:13*

But he that glorieth, let him glory in the Lord.

For not he that commendeth himself approved, but whom the Lord commendeth. *2 Corinthians 10:17–18*

And he said unto them, Ye are they which justify yourselves before men; but God knoweth your hearts: for that which is highly esteemed among men is abomination in the sight of God. *Luke 16:15*

Let another man praise thee, and not thine own mouth; a stranger, and not thine own lips.   ❧ *Proverbs 27:2*

Thou hast rebuked the proud that are cursed, which do err from thy commandments.   ❧ *Psalm 119:21*

He that is of a proud heart stirreth up strife: but he that putteth his trust in the Lord shall be made fat.

He that trusteth in his own heart is a fool: but whoso walketh wisely, he shall be delivered.

❧ *Proverbs 28:25–26*

How can ye believe, which receive honour one of another, and seek not the honour that cometh from God only?

❧ *John 5:44*

And he sat down, and called the twelve, and saith unto them, If any man desire to be first, the same shall be last of all, and servant of all.   ❧ *Mark 9:35*

Prisoners

But thus saith the Lord, Even the captives of the mighty shall be taken away, and the prey of the terrible shall be delivered: for I will contend with him that contendeth with thee, and I will save thy children.

❦ *Isaiah 49:25*

If any of thine be driven out unto the outmost parts of heaven, from thence will the Lord thy God gather thee, and from thence will he fetch thee.

❦ *Deuteronomy 30:4*

For the Lord heareth the poor, and despiseth not his prisoners.

❦ *Psalm 69:33*

He brought them out of darkness and the shadow of death, and brake their bands in sunder.

❦ *Psalm 107:14*

Which executeth judgment for the oppressed: which giveth food to the hungry. The Lord looseth the prisoners.

❦ *Psalm 146:7*

God setteth the solitary in families: he bringeth out those which are bound with chains: but the rebellious dwell in a dry land.

❦ *Psalm 68:6*

Protection, God's

The name of the Lord is a strong tower: the righteous runneth into it, and is safe.   ❦ *Proverbs 18:10*

At destruction and famine thou shalt laugh: neither shalt thou be afraid of the beasts of the earth.   ❦ *Job 5:22*

And thou shalt be secure, because there is hope; yea, thou shalt dig about thee, and thou shalt take thy rest in safety.

Also thou shalt lie down, and none shall make thee afraid; yea, many shall make suit unto thee.

❦ *Job 11:18–19*

The Lord shall preserve thee from all evil: he shall preserve thy soul.

The Lord shall preserve thy going out and thy coming in from this time forth, and even for evermore.

❦ *Psalm 121:7–8*

When thou liest down, thou shalt not be afraid: yea, thou shalt lie down, and thy sleep shall be sweet.

❦ *Proverbs 3:24*

And who is he that will harm you, if ye be followers of that which is good?   ❦ *1 Peter 3:13*

The beloved of the Lord shall dwell in safety by him; and the Lord shall cover him all the day long, and he shall dwell between his shoulders.

❦ *Deuteronomy 33:12*

He shall not be afraid of evil tidings: his heart is fixed, trusting in the Lord. 		❦ *Psalm 112:7*

Because thou hast made the Lord, which is my refuge, even the most High, thy habitation;

There shall no evil befall thee, neither shall any plague come nigh thy dwelling. 		❦ *Psalm 91:9–10*

But now thus saith the Lord that created thee, O Jacob, and he that formed thee, O Israel, Fear not: for I have redeemed thee, I have called thee by thy name; thou art mine.

When thou passest through the waters, I will be with thee; and through the rivers, they shall not overflow thee: when thou walkest through the fire, thou shalt not be burned; neither shall the flame kindle upon thee.

❦ *Isaiah 43:1–2*

And they shall no more be a prey to the heathen, neither shall the beast of the land devour them; but they shall dwell safely, and none shall make them afraid.

❦ *Ezekiel 34:28*

But whoso hearkeneth unto me shall dwell safely, and shall be quiet from fear of evil. 		❦ *Proverbs 1:33*

I will both lay me down in peace, and sleep: for thou, Lord, only makest me dwell in safety. 		❦ *Psalm 4:8*

The Lord is my light and my salvation; whom shall I fear? the Lord is the strength of my life; of whom shall I be afraid? 		❦ *Psalm 27:1*

Repentance

The time is fulfilled, and the kingdom of God is at hand: repent ye, and believe the gospel. ❦ *Mark 1:15*

And they went out, and preached that men should repent. ❦ *Mark 6:12*

The Lord is nigh unto them that are of a broken heart; and saveth such as be of a contrite spirit. ❦ *Psalm 34:18*

He healeth the broken in heart, and bindeth up their wounds. ❦ *Psalm 147:3*

If iniquity be in thine hand, put it far away, and let not wickedness dwell in thy tabernacles.

For then shalt thou lift up thy face without spot; yea, thou shalt be stedfast, and shalt not fear. ❦ *Job 11:14–15*

But if the wicked will turn from all his sins that he hath committed, and keep all my statutes, and do that which is lawful and right, he shall surely live, he shall not die.

All his transgressions that he hath committed, they shall not be mentioned unto him: in his righteousness that he hath done he shall live. ❦ *Ezekiel 18:21–22*

For I am not come to call the righteous, but sinners to repentance. ❦ *Matthew 9:13*

Righteousness

For the Lord God is a sun and shield: the Lord will give grace and glory: no good thing will he withhold from them that walk uprightly. ❧ *Psalm 84:11*

The young lions do lack, and suffer hunger: but they that seek the Lord shall not want any good thing.
❧ *Psalm 34:10*

The fear of the wicked, it shall come upon him: but the desire of the righteous shall be granted.
❧ *Proverbs 10:24*

Evil pursueth sinners: but to the righteous good shall be repayed. ❧ *Proverbs 13:21*

A good man obtaineth favour of the Lord: but a man of wicked devices will he condemn. ❧ *Proverbs 12:2*

But seek ye first the kingdom of God, and his righteousness; and all these things shall be added unto you.
❧ *Matthew 6:33*

He that trusteth in his riches shall fall: but the righteous shall flourish as a branch. ❧ *Proverbs 11:28*

So that a man shall say, Verily there is a reward for the righteous. ❧ *Psalm 58:11*

For thou, Lord, wilt bless the righteous; with favour wilt thou compass him as with a shield. *Psalm 5:12*

Salvation belongeth unto the Lord: thy blessing is upon thy people. *Psalm 3:8*

Whether Paul, or Apollos, or Cephas, or the world, or life, or death, or things present, or things to come; all are yours;
And ye are Christ's; and Christ is God's.
1 Corinthians 3:22–23

He that spared not his own Son, but delivered him up for us all, how shall he not with him also freely give us all things? Romans 8:32

Say ye to the righteous, that it shall be well with him: for they shall eat the fruit of their doings. *Isaiah 3:10*

Surely goodness and mercy shall follow me all the days of my life: and I will dwell in the house of the Lord for ever. *Psalm 23:6*

Salvation

Jesus answered and said unto him, Verily, verily, I say unto thee, Except a man be born again, he cannot see the kingdom of God.

Nicodemus saith unto him, How can a man be born when he is old? can he enter the second time into his mother's womb, and be born?

Jesus answered, Verily, verily, I say unto thee, Except a man be born of water and of the Spirit, he cannot enter into the kingdom of God.

That which is born of the flesh is flesh; and that which is born of the Spirit is spirit.

Marvel not that I said unto thee, Ye must be born again. ❦ *John 3:3–7*

Therefore if any man be in Christ, he is a new creature: old things are passed away; behold, all things are become new. ❦ *2 Corinthians 5:17*

For he hath made him to be sin for us, who knew no sin; that we might be made the righteousness of God in him. ❦ *2 Corinthians 5:21*

And you hath he quickened, who were dead in trespasses and sins. ❦ *Ephesians 2:1*

For this is good and acceptable in the sight of God our Saviour;

Who will have all men to be saved, and to come unto the knowledge of the truth. ❦ *1 Timothy 2:3–4*

My little children, these things write I unto you, that ye sin not. And if any man sin, we have an advocate with the Father, Jesus Christ the righteous:

And he is the propitiation for our sins: and not for ours only, but also for the sins of the whole world.

❦ *1 John 2:1–2*

And you, being dead in your sins and the uncircumcision of your flesh, hath he quickened together with him, having forgiven you all trespasses.

❦ *Colossians 2:13*

This is a faithful saying and worthy of all acceptation.

For therefore we both labour and suffer reproach, because we trust in the living God, who is the Saviour of all men, specially of those that believe.

❦ *1 Timothy 4:9–10*

But not as the offence, so also is the free gift. For if through the offence of one many be dead, much more the grace of God, and the gift by grace, which is by one man, Jesus Christ, hath abounded unto many.

❦ *Romans 5:15*

But after that the kindness and love of God our Saviour toward man appeared,

Not by works of righteousness which we have done, but according to his mercy he saved us, by the washing of regeneration, and renewing of the Holy Ghost;

Which he shed on us abundantly through Jesus Christ our Saviour.   ❦ *Titus 3:4–6*

But as many as received him, to them gave he power to become the sons of God, even to them that believe on his name:

Which were born, not of blood, nor of the will of the flesh, nor of the will of man, but of God.

John 1:12–13

Seeking God

The Lord is with you, while ye be with him; and if ye seek him, he will be found of you; but if ye forsake him, he will forsake you. ❦ *2 Chronicles 15:2*

Sow to yourselves in righteousness, reap in mercy; break up your fallow ground: for it is time to seek the Lord, till he come and rain righteousness upon you.

❦ *Hosea 10:12*

But without faith it is impossible to please him: for he that cometh to God must believe that he is, and that he is a rewarder of them that diligently seek him.

❦ *Hebrews 11:6*

That they should seek the Lord, if haply they might feel after him, and find him, though he be not far from every one of us. ❦ *Acts 17:27*

The Lord is good unto them that wait for him, to the soul that seeketh him. ❦ *Lamentations 3:25*

But if from thence thou shalt seek the Lord thy God, thou shalt find him, if thou seek him with all thy heart and with all thy soul. ❦ *Deuteronomy 4:29*

The hand of our God is upon all them for good that seek him; but his power and his wrath is against all them that forsake him. ❦ *Ezra 8:22*

For thus saith the Lord unto the house of Israel, Seek ye me, and ye shall live. ❦ *Amos 5:4*

And thou, Solomon my son, know thou the God of thy father, and serve him with a perfect heart and with a willing mind: for the Lord searcheth all hearts, and understandeth all the imaginations of the thoughts: if thou seek him, he will be found of thee; but if thou forsake him, he will cast thee off for ever. ❦ *1 Chronicles 28:9*

If thou wouldest seek unto God betimes, and make thy supplication to the Almighty;

If thou wert pure and upright; surely now he would awake for thee, and make the habitation of thy righteousness prosperous. ❦ *Job 8:5–6*

And they that know thy name will put their trust in thee: for thou, Lord, hast not forsaken them that seek thee.
❦ *Psalm 9:10*

And ye shall seek me, and find me, when ye shall search for me with all your heart. ❦ *Jeremiah 29:13*

Self-Denial

Then said Jesus unto his disciples, If any man will come after me, let him deny himself, and take up his cross, and follow me.

For whosoever will save his life shall lose it: and whosoever will lose his life for my sake shall find it.

For what is a man profited, if he shall gain the whole world, and lose his own soul? or what shall a man give in exchange for his soul? ❦ *Matthew 16:24–26*

Therefore, brethren, we are debtors, not to the flesh, to live after the flesh.

For if ye live after the flesh, ye shall die: but if ye through the Spirit do mortify the deeds of the body, ye shall live. ❦ *Romans 8:12–13*

For the grace of God that bringeth salvation hath appeared to all men,

Teaching us that, denying ungodliness and worldly lusts, we should live soberly, righteously, and godly, in this present world. ❦ *Titus 2:11–12*

But I say unto you, That ye resist not evil: but whosoever shall smite thee on thy right cheek, turn to him the other also.

And if any man will sue thee at the law, and take away thy coat, let him have thy cloak also.

And whosoever shall compel thee to go a mile, go with him twain. ❦ *Matthew 5:39–41*

And he said unto them, Verily I say unto you, There is no man that hath left house, or parents, or brethren, or wife, or children, for the kingdom of God's sake,

Who shall not receive manifold more in this present time, and in the world to come life everlasting.

❦ *Luke 18:29–30*

And they that are Christ's have crucified the flesh with the affections and lusts. ❦ *Galatians 5:24*

Self-Righteousness

Surely thou hast spoken in mine hearing, and I have heard the voice of thy words, saying,

I am clean without transgression, I am innocent; neither is there iniquity in me.   ❧ *Job 33:8–9*

Thinkest thou this to be right, that thou saidst, My righteousness is more than God's?   ❧ *Job 35:2*

Woe unto them that are wise in their own eyes, and prudent in their own sight!   ❧ *Isaiah 5:21*

Surely God will not hear vanity, neither will the Almighty regard it.   ❧ *Job 35:13*

Seest thou a man wise in his own conceit? there is more hope of a fool than of him.   ❧ *Proverbs 26:12*

But he that glorieth, let him glory in the Lord.

For not he that commendeth himself is approved, but whom the Lord commendeth.

    ❧ *2 Corinthians 10:17–18*

He that is of a proud heart stirreth up strife: but he that putteth his trust in the Lord shall be made fat.

He that trusteth in his own heart is a fool: but whoso walketh wisely, he shall be delivered.

    ❧ *Proverbs 28:25–26*

For if a man think himself to be something, when he is nothing, he deceiveth himself. ❦ *Galatians 6:3*

Let another man praise thee, and not thine own mouth; a stranger, and not thine own lips. ❦ *Proverbs 27:2*

Jesus said unto them, If ye were blind, ye should have no sin: but now ye say, We see; therefore your sin remaineth.
❦ *John 9:41*

But we are all as an unclean thing, and all our righteous-nesses are as filthy rags; and we all do fade as a leaf; and our iniquities, like the wind, have taken us away.
❦ *Isaiah 64:6*

And he said unto them, Ye are they which justify your-selves before men; but God knoweth your hearts: for that which is highly esteemed among men is abomination in the sight of God. ❦ *Luke 16:15*

Sexual Sins

Now the body is not for fornication, but for the Lord; and the Lord for the body. 🐝 *1 Corinthians 6:13*

Flee fornication. Every sin that a man doeth is without the body; but he that committeth fornication sinneth against his own body.

What? know ye not that your body is the temple of the Holy Ghost which is in you, which ye have of God, and ye are not your own?

For ye are bought with a price: therefore glorify God in your body, and in your spirit, which are God's.
🐝 *1 Corinthians 6:18–20*

There hath no temptation taken you but such as is common to man: but God is faithful, who will not suffer you to be tempted above that ye are able; but will with the temptation also make a way to escape, that ye may be able to bear it. 🐝 *1 Corinthians 10:13*

Now concerning the things whereof ye wrote unto me: It is good for a man not to touch a woman.
🐝 *1 Corinthians 7:1*

I say therefore to the unmarried and widows, It is good for them if they abide even as I.

But if they cannot contain, let them marry: for it is better to marry than to burn. 🐝 *1 Corinthians 7:8–9*

Nevertheless he that standeth stedfast in his heart, having no necessity, but hath power over his own will, and hath so decreed in his heart that he will keep his virgin, doeth well.   ❦ *1 Corinthians 7:37*

Marriage is honourable in all, and the bed undefiled: but whoremongers and adulterers God will judge.

                                            ❦ *Hebrews 13:4*

These are they which were not defiled with women; for they are virgins. These are they which follow the Lamb whithersoever he goeth. These were redeemed from among men, being the firstfruits unto God and to the Lamb.   ❦ *Revelation 14:4*

For this is the will of God, even your sanctification, that ye should abstain from fornication.

                                     ❦ *1 Thessalonians 4:3*

Know ye not that your bodies are the members of Christ? shall I then take the members of Christ, and make them the members of an harlot? God forbid.

                                     ❦ *1 Corinthians 6:15*

Who can find a virtuous woman? for her price is far above rubies.   ❦ *Proverbs 31:10*

The Lord knoweth how to deliver the godly out of temptations, and to reserve the unjust unto the day of judgment to be punished.   ❦ *2 Peter 2:9*

Blessed is the man that endureth temptation: for when he is tried, he shall receive the crown of life, which the Lord hath promised to them that love him.

🐾 *James 1:12*

For in that he himself hath suffered being tempted, he is able to succour them that are tempted.

🐾 *Hebrews 2:18*

For we have not an high priest which cannot be touched with the feeling of our infirmities; but was in all points tempted like as we are, yet without sin.

Let us therefore come boldly unto the throne of grace, that we may obtain mercy, and find grace to help in time of need.   🐾 *Hebrews 4:15–16*

Shame

For the scripture saith, Whosoever believeth on him shall not be ashamed. *Romans 10:11*

Then shall I not be ashamed, when I have respect unto all thy commandments. *Psalm 119:6*

And hope maketh not ashamed; because the love of God is shed abroad in our hearts by the Holy Ghost which is given unto us. *Romans 5:5*

For the which cause I also suffer these things: nevertheless I am not ashamed: for I know whom I have believed, and am persuaded that he is able to keep that which I have committed unto him against that day.

2 Timothy 1:12

As it is written, Behold, I lay in Sion a stumblingstone and rock of offence: and whosoever believeth on him shall not be ashamed. *Romans 9:33*

Study to shew thyself approved unto God, a workman that needeth not to be ashamed, rightly dividing the word of truth. *2 Timothy 2:15*

Let my heart be sound in thy statutes; that I be not ashamed. *Psalm 119:80*

Yet if any man suffer as a Christian, let him not be ashamed; but let him glorify God on this behalf.

1 Peter 4:16

Sickness

Is any sick among you? let him call for the elders of the church; and let them pray over him, anointing him with oil in the name of the Lord:

And the prayer of faith shall save the sick, and the Lord shall raise him up; and if he have committed sins, they shall be forgiven him.

Confess your faults one to another, and pray one for another, that ye may be healed. The effectual fervent prayer of a righteous man availeth much.

❧ *James 5:14–16*

And when he was come into the house, the blind men came to him: and Jesus saith unto them, Believe ye that I am able to do this? They said unto him, Yea, Lord.

Then touched he their eyes, saying, According to your faith be it unto you.

And their eyes were opened.

❧ *Matthew 9:28–30*

Heal me, O Lord, and I shall be healed; save me, and I shall be saved: for thou art my praise.

❧ *Jeremiah 17:14*

But that ye may know that the Son of man hath power on earth to forgive sins, (then saith he to the sick of the palsy,) Arise, take up thy bed, and go unto thine house.

And he arose, and departed to his house.

❧ *Matthew 9:6–7*

And Jesus went about all Galilee, teaching in their synagogues, and preaching the gospel of the kingdom, and healing all manner of sickness and all manner of disease among the people.

And his fame went throughout all Syria: and they brought unto him all sick people that were taken with divers diseases and torments, and those which were possessed with devils, and those which were lunatic, and those that had the palsy; and he healed them.

❦ *Matthew 4:23–24*

For I will restore health unto thee, and I will heal thee of thy wounds, saith the Lord. ❦ *Jeremiah 30:17*

And ye shall serve the Lord your God, and he shall bless thy bread, and thy water; and I will take sickness away from the midst of thee. ❦ *Exodus 23:25*

Who his own self bare our sins in his own body on the tree, that we, being dead to sins, should live unto righteousness: by whose stripes ye were healed.

❦ *1 Peter 2:24*

But he was wounded for our transgressions, he was bruised for our iniquities: the chastisement of our peace was upon him; and with his stripes we are healed.

❦ *Isaiah 53:5*

Sin, Freedom from

Then will I sprinkle clean water upon you, and ye shall be clean: from all your filthiness, and from all your idols, will I cleanse you.

A new heart also will I give you, and a new spirit will I put within you: and I will take away the stony heart out of your flesh, and I will give you an heart of flesh.

❦ *Ezekiel 36:25–26*

To him give all the prophets witness, that through his name whosoever believeth in him shall receive remission of sins. ❦ *Acts 10:43*

Knowing this, that our old man is crucified with him, that the body of sin might be destroyed, that henceforth we should not serve sin.

For he that is dead is freed from sin.

❦ *Romans 6:6–7*

Therefore if any man be in Christ, he is a new creature: old things are passed away; behold, all things are become new. ❦ *2 Corinthians 5:17*

What shall we say then? Shall we continue in sin, that grace may abound?

God forbid. How shall we, that are dead to sin, live any longer therein? ❦ *Romans 6:1–2*

For sin shall not have dominion over you: for ye are not under the law, but under grace. ❦ *Romans 6:14*

Likewise reckon ye also yourselves to be dead indeed unto sin, but alive unto God through Jesus Christ our Lord. ❦ *Romans 6:11*

Sin, Redemption from

And she shall bring forth a son, and thou shalt call his name JESUS: for he shall save his people from their sins.
❦ *Matthew 1:21*

Be it known unto you therefore, men and brethren, that through this man is preached unto you the forgiveness of sins.
❦ *Acts 13:38*

Who gave himself for our sins, that he might deliver us from this present evil world, according to the will of God and our Father.
❦ *Galatians 1:4*

And if any man sin, we have an advocate with the Father, Jesus Christ the righteous:
And he is the propitiation for our sins: and not for ours only, but also for the sins of the whole world.
❦ *1 John 2:1–2*

Who his own self bare our sins in his own body on the tree, that we, being dead to sins, should live unto righteousness: by whose stripes ye were healed.
❦ *1 Peter 2:24*

This is a faithful saying, and worthy of all acceptation, that Christ Jesus came into the world to save sinners; of whom I am chief.
❦ *1 Timothy 1:15*

For by one offering he hath perfected for ever them that are sanctified.
❦ *Hebrews 10:14*

The next day John seeth Jesus coming unto him, and saith, Behold the Lamb of God, which taketh away the sin of the world. 			❦ *John 1:29*

But he was wounded for our transgressions, he was bruised for our iniquities: the chastisement of our peace was upon him; and with his stripes we are healed.

All we like sheep have gone astray; we have turned every one to his own way; and the Lord hath laid on him in the iniquity of us all. 			❦ *Isaiah 53:5–6*

In whom we have redemption through his blood, the forgiveness of sins, according to the riches of his grace.

❦ *Ephesians 1:7*

And ye know that he was manifested to take away our sins; and in him is no sin. 			❦ *1 John 3:5*

So Christ was once offered to bear the sins of many; and unto them that look for him shall he appear the second time without sin unto salvation. 			❦ *Hebrews 9:28*

For this is my blood of the new testament, which is shed for many for the remission of sins.

❦ *Matthew 26:28*

Slander and Reproach

Blessed are ye, when men shall revile you, and persecute you, and shall say all manner of evil against you falsely, for my sake.

Rejoice, and be exceeding glad: for great is your reward in heaven: for so persecuted they the prophets which were before you. ❦ *Matthew 5:11–12*

If ye be reproached for the name of Christ, happy are ye; for the spirit of glory and of God resteth upon you: on their part he is evil spoken of, but on your part he is glorified. ❦ *1 Peter 4:14*

He shall send from heaven, and save me from the reproach of him that would swallow me up. Selah. God shall send forth his mercy and his truth.

❦ *Psalm 57:3*

Hearken unto me, ye that know righteousness, the people in whose heart is my law; fear ye not the reproach of men, neither be ye afraid of their revilings.

❦ *Isaiah 51:7*

Thou shalt hide them in the secret of thy presence from the pride of man: thou shalt keep them secretly in a pavilion from the strife of tongues. ❦ *Psalm 31:20*

And he shall bring forth thy righteousness as the light, and thy judgment as the noonday. ❦ *Psalm 37:6*

Thou shalt be hid from the scourge of the tongue: neither shalt thou be afraid of destruction when it cometh.

❦ *Job 5:21*

Success

In the house of the righteous is much treasure: but in the revenues of the wicked is trouble.   ❦ *Proverbs 15:6*

By humility and the fear of the Lord are riches, and honour, and life.   ❦ *Proverbs 22:4*

And the Lord thy God will make thee plenteous in every work of thine hand, in the fruit of thy body, and in the fruit of thy cattle, and in the fruit of thy land, for good: for the Lord will again rejoice over thee for good, as he rejoiced over thy fathers.   ❦ *Deuteronomy 30:9*

And the Lord shall make thee plenteous in goods, in the fruit of thy body, and in the fruit of thy cattle, and in the fruit of thy ground, in the land which the Lord sware unto thy fathers to give thee.

The Lord shall open unto thee his good treasure, the heaven to give the rain unto thy land in his season, and to bless all the work of thine hand: and thou shalt lend unto many nations, and thou shalt not borrow.

And the Lord shall make thee the head, and not the tail; and thou shalt be above only, and thou shalt not beneath; if that thou hearken unto the commandments of the Lord thy God, which I command thee this day, to observe and to do them.   ❦ *Deuteronomy 28:11–13*

And also that every man should eat and drink, and enjoy the good of all his labour, it is the gift of God.
     ❦ *Ecclesiastes 3:13*

Every man also to whom God hath given riches and wealth, and hath given him power to eat thereof, and to take his portion, and to rejoice in his labour; this is the gift of God. *Ecclesiastes 5:19*

Then shall he give the rain of thy seed, that thou shalt sow the ground withal; and bread of the increase of the earth, and it shall be fat and plenteous: in that day shall thy cattle feed in large pastures. *Isaiah 30:23*

And he shall be like a tree planted by the rivers of water, that bringeth forth his fruit in his season; his leaf also shall not wither; and whatsoever he doeth shall prosper.
Psalm 1:3

Riches and honour are with me; yea, durable riches and righteousness.

My fruit is better than gold, yea, than fine gold; and my revenue than choice silver. *Proverbs 8:18–19*

Wealth and riches shall be in his house: and his righteousness endureth for ever. *Psalm 112:3*

And I will send grass in thy fields for thy cattle, that thou mayest eat and be full. *Deuteronomy 11:15*

Then shalt thou lay up gold as dust, and the gold of Ophir as the stones of the brooks.

Yea, the Almighty shall be thy defence, and thou shalt have plenty of silver. *Job 22:24–25*

Thou shalt also decree a thing, and it shall be established unto thee: and the light shall shine upon thy ways.

❦ Job 22:28

For thou shalt eat the labour of thine hands: happy shalt thou be, and it shall be well with thee.

❦ Psalm 128:2

And they shall build houses, and inhabit them; and they shall plant vineyards, and eat the fruit of them.

They shall not build, and another inhabit; they shall not plant, and another eat: for as the days of a tree are the days of my people, and mine elect shall long enjoy the work of their hands.

They shall not labor in vain, nor bring forth for trouble; for they are the seed of the blessed of the Lord, and their offspring with them. *❦ Isaiah 65:21–23*

And all these blessings shall come on thee, and overtake thee, if thou shalt hearken unto the voice of the Lord thy God.

Blessed shalt thou be in the city, and blessed shalt thou be in the field.

Blessed shall be the fruit of thy body, and the fruit of thy ground, and the fruit of thy cattle, the increase of thy kine, and the flocks of thy sheep.

Blessed shall be thy basket and thy store.

Blessed shalt thou be when thou comest in, and blessed shalt thou be when thou goest out.

❦ Deuteronomy 28:2–6

Trust

God is our refuge and strength, a very present help in trouble.

Therefore will not we fear, though the earth be removed, and though the mountains be carried into the midst of the sea. ❦ *Psalm 46:1–2*

For the Lord God is a sun and shield: the Lord will give grace and glory: no good thing will he withhold from them that walk uprightly.

O Lord of hosts, blessed is the man that trusteth in thee. ❦ *Psalm 84:11–12*

Trust in the Lord, and do good; so shalt thou dwell in the land, and verily thou shalt be fed.

Delight thyself also in the Lord; and he shall give thee the desires of thine heart.

Commit thy way unto the Lord; trust also in him; and he shall bring it to pass. ❦ *Psalm 37:3–5*

Trust in the Lord with all thine heart; and lean not unto thine own understanding.

In all thy ways acknowledge him, and he shall direct thy paths. ❦ *Proverbs 3:5–6*

Fear not, little flock; for it is your Father's good pleasure to give you the kingdom. ❦ *Luke 12:32*

Casting all your care upon him; for he careth for you.
❦ *1 Peter 5:7*

They that trust in the Lord shall be as mount Zion, which cannot be removed, but abideth for ever.

❧ *Psalm 125:1*

Therefore take no thought, saying, What shall we eat? or, What shall we drink? or, Wherewithal shall we be clothed?

(For after all these things do the Gentiles seek:) for your heavenly Father knoweth that ye have need of all these things. ❧ *Matthew 6:31–32*

Blessed is that man that maketh the Lord his trust.

❧ *Psalm 40:4*

Wisdom

If any of you lack wisdom, let him ask of God, that giveth to all men liberally, and upbraideth not; and it shall be given him.   ❦ *James 1:5*

And he will teach us of his ways, and we will walk in his paths.   ❦ *Isaiah 2:3*

I will instruct thee and teach thee in the way which thou shalt go: I will guide thee with mine eye.

❦ *Psalm 32:8*

For God giveth to a man that is good in his sight wisdom, and knowledge, and joy.   ❦ *Ecclesiastes 2:26*

I will bless the Lord, who hath given me counsel: my reins also instruct me in the night seasons.

❦ *Psalm 16:7*

Then shalt thou understand the fear of the Lord, and find the knowledge of God.

For the Lord giveth wisdom: out of his mouth cometh knowledge and understanding.

He layeth up sound wisdom for righteous: he is a buckler to them that walk uprightly.

❦ *Proverbs 2:5–7*

Evil men understand not judgment: but they that seek the Lord understand all things.   ❦ *Proverbs 28:5*

And we know that the Son of God is come, and hath given us an understanding, that we may know him that is true, and we are in him that is true, even in his Son Jesus Christ. This is the true God, and eternal life.

❦ *1 John 5:20*

For God, who commanded the light to shine out of darkness, hath shined in our hearts, to give the light of the knowledge of the glory of God in the face of Jesus Christ.

❦ *2 Corinthians 4:6*

Behold, thou desirest truth in the inward parts: and in the hidden part thou shalt make me to know wisdom.

❦ *Psalm 51:6*

Word of God

For I am not ashamed of the gospel of Christ: for it is the power of God unto salvation to every one that believeth.

❧ *Romans 1:16*

Blessed is he that readeth, and they that hear the words of this prophecy, and keep those things which are written therein: for the time is at hand.

❧ *Revelation 1:3*

We have also a more sure word of prophecy; whereunto ye do well that ye take heed, as unto a light that shineth in a dark place, until the day dawn, and the day star arise in your hearts.   ❧ *2 Peter 1:19*

For the word of God is quick, and powerful, and sharper than any two-edged sword, piercing even to the dividing asunder of soul and spirit, and of the joints and marrow, and is a discerner of the thoughts and intents of the heart.

❧ *Hebrews 4:12*

Search the scriptures; for in them ye think ye have eternal life: and they are they which testify of me.

❧ *John 5:39*

For the commandment is a lamp; and the law is light; and reproofs of instruction are the way of life.

❧ *Proverbs 6:23*

The entrance of thy words giveth light; it giveth under-standing unto the simple. ❦ *Psalm 119:130*

The holy scriptures, which are able to make thee wise unto salvation through faith which is in Christ Jesus.

All scripture is given by inspiration of God, and is profitable for doctrine, for reproof, for correction, for instruction in righteousness. ❦ *2 Timothy 3:15–16*

So then faith cometh by hearing, and hearing by the word of God. ❦ *Romans 10:17*

As newborn babes, desire the sincere milk of the word, that ye may grow thereby. ❦ *1 Peter 2:2*

Therefore shall ye lay up these my words in your heart and in your soul, and bind them for a sign upon your hand, that they may be as frontlets between your eyes.
❦ *Deuteronomy 11:18*

This book of the law shall not depart out of thy mouth; but thou shalt meditate therein day and night, that thou mayest observe to do according to all that is written therein: for then thou shalt make thy way prosperous, and then thou shalt have good success. ❦ *Joshua 1:8*

And now, brethren, I commend you to God, and to the word of his grace, which is able to build you up, and to give you an inheritance among all them which are sanctified.
❦ *Acts 20:32*

Thy word is thy lamp unto my feet, and a light unto my path. 🌼 *Psalm 119:105*

Wherefore lay apart all filthiness and superfluity of naughtiness, and receive with meekness the engrafted word, which is able to save your souls.

But be ye doers of the word, and not hearers only, deceiving your own selves.

For if any be a hearer of the word, and not a doer, he is like unto a man beholding his natural face in a glass:

For he beholdeth himself, and goeth his way, and straightway forgetteth what manner of man he was.

But whoso looketh into the perfect law of liberty, and continueth therein, he being not a forgetful hearer, but a doer of the work, this man shall be blessed in his deed. 🌼 *James 1:21–25*

Being born again, not of corruptible seed, but of incorruptible, by the word of God, which liveth and abideth for ever. 🌼 *1 Peter 1:23*

Work

And God blessed the seventh day, and sanctified it: because that in it he had rested from all his work which God created and made.   🐦 *Genesis 2:3*

The Lord shall open unto thee his good treasure, the heaven to give the rain unto thy land in his season, and to bless all the work of thine hand: and thou shalt lend unto many nations, and thou shalt not borrow.
🐦 *Deuteronomy 28:12*

Be ye strong therefore, and let not your hands be weak: for your work shall be rewarded.   🐦 *2 Chronicles 15:7*

And in every work that he began in the service of the house of God, and in the law, and in the commandments, to seek his God, he did it with all his heart, and prospered.   🐦 *2 Chronicles 31:21*

Even a child is known by his doings, whether his work be pure, and whether it be right.   🐦 *Proverbs 20:11*

Jesus saith unto them, My meat is to do the will of him that sent me, and to finish his work.   🐦 *John 4:34*

Then said they unto him, What shall we do, that we might work the works of God?
Jesus answered and said unto them, This is the work of God, that ye believe on him whom he hath sent.
🐦 *John 6: 28–29*

I have glorified thee on the earth: I have finished the work which thou gavest me to do.

And now, O Father, glorify thou me with thine own self with the glory which I had with thee before the world was. ❦ *John 17:4–5*

Therefore, my beloved brethren, be ye stedfast, unmoveable, always abounding in the work of the Lord, forasmuch as ye know that your labour is not in vain in the Lord. ❦ *1 Corinthians 15:58*

That ye might walk worthy of the Lord unto all pleasing, being fruitful in every good work, and increasing in the knowledge of God. ❦ *Colossians 1:10*

For we hear that there are some which walk among you disorderly, working not at all, but are busybodies.

Now them that are such we command and exhort by our Lord Jesus Christ, that with quietness they work, and eat their own bread. ❦ *2 Thessalonians 3:11–12*

For God is not unrighteous to forget your work and labour of love, which ye have shewed toward his name, in that ye have ministered to the saints, and do minister.

And we desire that every one of you do shew the same diligence to the full assurance of hope unto the end.

❦ *Hebrews 6:10–11*

Except the Lord build the house, they labour in vain that build it: except the Lord keep the city, the watchman waketh but in vain. ❦ *Psalm 127:1*

In all labour there is profit: but the talk of the lips tendeth only to penury. 🐝 *Proverbs 14:23*

Let him that stole steal no more: but rather let him labour, working with his hands the thing which is good, that he may have to give to him that needeth. 🐝 *Ephesians 4:28*

Come unto me, all ye that labour and are heavy laden, and I will give you rest. 🐝 *Matthew 11:28*

Worry

Be careful for nothing; but in every thing by prayer and supplication with thanksgiving let your requests be made known unto God.

And the peace of God, which passeth all understanding, shall keep your hearts and minds through Christ Jesus. ❦ *Philippians 4:6–7*

God is our refuge and strength, a very present help in trouble.

Therefore will not we fear, though the earth be removed, and though the mountains be carried into the midst of the sea;

Though the waters thereof roar and be troubled, though the mountains shake with the swelling thereof.
❦ *Psalm 46:1–3*

For he shall be as a tree planted by the waters, and that spreadeth out her roots by the river, and shall not see when heat cometh, but her leaf shall be green; and shall not be careful in the year of drought, neither shall cease from yielding fruit. ❦ *Jeremiah 17:8*

And Jesus answered and said unto her, Martha, Martha, thou art careful and troubled about many things:

But one thing is needful: and Mary hath chosen that good part, which shall not be taken away from her.
❦ *Luke 10:41–42*

But my God shall supply all your need according to his riches in glory by Christ Jesus. 🎕 *Philippians 4:19*

The Lord also will be a refuge for the oppressed, a refuge in times of trouble.

And they that know thy name will put their trust in thee: for thou, Lord, hast not forsaken them that seek thee. 🎕 *Psalm 9:9–10*

Thou art my hiding place; thou shalt preserve me from trouble; thou shalt compass me about with songs of deliverance. 🎕 *Psalm 32:7*

He shall call upon me, and I will answer him: I will be with him in trouble; I will deliver him, and honour him. 🎕 *Psalm 91:15*

We are troubled on every side, yet not distressed; we are perplexed, but not in despair;

Persecuted, but not forsaken; cast down, but not destroyed. 🎕 *2 Corinthians 4:8–9*

And we know that all things work together for good to them that love God, to them who are the called according to his purpose. 🎕 *Romans 8:28*

And the work of righteousness shall be peace; and the effect of righteousness quietness and assurance for ever. 🎕 *Isaiah 32:17*

Worship

All the earth shall worship thee, and shall sing unto thee; they shall sing to thy name. ❦ *Psalm 66:4*

O come, let us worship and bow down: let us kneel before the Lord our maker.

For he is our God; and we are the people of his pasture, and the sheep of his hand. ❦ *Psalm 95:6–7*

Exalt the Lord our God, and worship at his holy hill; for the Lord our God is holy. ❦ *Psalm 99:9*

Now when Jesus was born in Bethlehem of Judaea in the days of Herod the king, behold, there came wise men from the east to Jerusalem,

Saying, Where is he that is born King of the Jews? for we have seen his star in the east, and are come to worship him.

❦ *Matthew 2:1–2*

God is a Spirit: and they that worship him must worship him in spirit and in truth. ❦ *John 4:24*

The four and twenty elders fall down before him that sat on the throne, and worship him that liveth for ever and ever, and cast their crowns before the throne, saying,

Thou art worthy, O Lord, to receive glory and honour and power: for thou hast created all things, and for thy pleasure they are and were created.

❦ *Revelation 4:10–11*

All nations whom thou hast made shall come and worship before thee, O Lord; and shall glorify thy name.

🍎 *Psalm 86:9*

Who shall not fear thee, O Lord, and glorify thy name? for thou only art holy: for all nations shall come and worship before thee; for thy judgments are made manifest.

🍎 Revelation 15:4

And I fell at his feet to worship him. And he said unto me, See thou do it not: I am thy fellow-servant, and of thy brethren that have the testimony of Jesus: worship God: for the testimony of Jesus is the spirit of prophecy.

🍎 *Revelation 19:10*

And the devil said unto him, All this power will I give thee, and the glory of them: for that is delivered unto me; and to whomsoever I will I give it.

If thou therefore wilt worship me, all shall be thine.

And Jesus answered and said unto him, Get thee behind me, Satan: for it is written, Thou shalt worship the Lord thy God, and him only shalt thou serve.

🍎 *Luke 4:6–8*

And, behold, there came a leper and worshipped him, saying, Lord, if thou wilt, thou canst make me clean.

And Jesus put forth his hand, and touched him, saying, I will; be thou clean. And immediately his leprosy was cleansed. 🍎 *Matthew 8:2–3*

I will praise the Lord according to his righteousness: and will sing praise to the name of the Lord most high.

❦ *Psalm 7:17*

Shadrach, Meshach, and Abednego, answered and said to the king, O Nebuchadnezzar, we are not careful to answer thee in this matter.

If it be so, our God whom we serve is able to deliver us from the burning fiery furnace, and he will deliver us out of thine hand, O king.

But if not, be it known unto thee, O king, that we will not serve thy gods, nor worship the golden image which thou hast set up. ❦ *Daniel 3:16–18*

And the four and twenty elders, which sat before God on their seats, fell upon their faces, and worshipped God,

Saying, We give thee thanks, O Lord God Almighty, which art, and wast, and art to come; because thou hast taken to thee thy great power, and hast reigned. ❦ *Revelation 11:16–17*

NOTES

NOTES

NOTES

NOTES

NOTES

NOTES

Inspirational Library

Beautiful purse/pocket-size editions of Christian classics bound in flexible leatherette. These books make thoughtful gifts for everyone on your list, including yourself!

When I'm on My Knees   The highly popular collection of devotional thoughts on prayer, especially for women.
      Flexible Leatherette. $4.97

The Bible Promise Book for Men   Promises from God's Word arranged by topic. What does God promise about matters like: Anger, Duty, Forgiveness, Mercy, Power, Self-Control, and Wisdom? Find out in this book!
      Flexible Leatherette. $4.97

Daily Wisdom for Women   A daily devotional for women seeking biblical wisdom to apply to their lives. Scripture taken from the New American Standard Version of the Bible.
      Flexible Leatherette. $5.97

A Gentle Spirit   With an emphasis on personal spiritual development, this daily devotional for women draws from the best writings of Christian female authors.
      Flexible Leatherette. $5.97

Available wherever books are sold.
Or order from:

Barbour Publishing, Inc.
P.O. Box 719
Uhrichsville, OH 44683
www.barbourbooks.com

If you order by mail, add $2.00 to your order for shipping.
Prices are subject to change without notice.